Your Lawsuit

UNDERSTANDING THE SCRAPES, SCRATCHES,
AND INDIGNITIES OF THE CALIFORNIA
LITIGATION PROCESS FROM START TO FINISH

Keith A. Davidson &
Stewart R. Albertson

Table of Contents

Section Five—Other Pretrial Concerns

Section Six—The Trial Phase

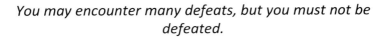

You may encounter many defeats, but you must not be defeated.

—Maya Angelou

A "Friendly Warning" on the Reality of Lawsuits

On December 5, 2000, Keith A. Davidson became a member of the California State Bar Association, a ticket to practicing law in the State of California. Stewart Albertson followed suit on December 27, 2002 in Louisiana and then June 1, 2004 in California. Becoming licensed to practice law is where our journey began in earnest. You see, lawyers don't know much when they first become lawyers. Law school only teaches so much, and it lacks the practical application of law. There's an old saying that law graduates know everything, but, unfortunately, they'd don't know anything else.

The law is never applied in a vacuum. It takes legal rules, judicial decisions, the messy facts of each case, and most importantly people. People are the law—not laws. Laws provide guidance, people provide application. Every lawsuit has a mix of people that includes the clients, the family of the clients who want to be involved, the clients' lawyer (or lawyers), the opposing parties and their lawyers, the judge, the court personnel, witnesses, entities that have documents, experts, and many others. A lawsuit is nothing more than a group of people coming together to resolve a problem. Of course, in our adversarial judicial system, people don't "come together" in a positive way necessarily. But they come together nonetheless; and a resolution is reached eventually.

Lawyers must learn to navigate a case through this maze of people. And that is where the practical education begins. Right after law school, without any warning, the reality of the judicial system hits us square in the face. It can be a tough lesson, but a necessary one.

In the following pages we are going to give you some basic understanding of the legal process you—as the litigant—are about to enter. You too will have to navigate this process.

But before we begin we thought it might be helpful if we spared you from being hit in the face with this reality: lawsuits are chaotic. Prepare for some, or much, chaos.

That's why it helps to have an experienced guide with you on your journey. That's what a good lawyer is, after all—an experienced guide. If you were going to travel down the Amazon River in South America, and had never done so before, wouldn't you want to hire an experienced guide to show you the way? Experience counts. In fact, experience can mean the difference between life and death in the wilderness— what will you encounter, how will you handle different situations, what can you eat if you must forage for food, how will you survive in the elements?

Of course, even the most experienced guide cannot guarantee your survival; failure is always an option. People climb Mount Everest with experienced guides, but some of the climbers, and guides too for that matter, still perish. The same is true in lawsuits—not the "perish" part, but the "no-guarantee-of-success" part.

Failure is always an option in every lawsuit. We have seen great cases lose, and terrible cases win at trial. Sometimes people win in spite of their mistakes, or lose in spite of their best efforts. You must be prepared for alternate outcomes. It can seem like a bit of a crapshoot. But not really. In fact, most cases will probably be resolved close to what is objectively reasonable for the case. That doesn't mean you will like the result or think it fair. But it probably is objectively reasonable under the circumstances.

Again, it all comes down to people. The law is not black and white because people apply the facts of your case to the law, and people are not black and white. People have viewpoints, emotions, and their own past experiences that will influence how they view your case.

Law is a people business. As you begin your journey into your lawsuit, take some advice from those of us who spend our professional lives in this chaotic world: be flexible, be resilient, be persistent; and with that you will succeed. In the words of Kenny Rogers, "You have to know when to hold 'em, and know when to fold 'em."

Introduction—Welcome to Your Lawsuit. Don't Forget to Buckle Up

If you have never been involved in a lawsuit before, you may be surprised at just how confusing (and slow) our court system can be. Lawsuits in America proceed on the basis of due process of law. Due process simply means that every party must be given a fair chance to present evidence in court before a judge or jury. Sounds simple, but that process of fairness takes time because, in California at least, there are far more lawsuits filed than judges or juries to decide them.

Further, if you are heading into trial and your case depends on the strength of your evidence, don't you want to find the best evidence you can to support your case? Of course you do, and that brings us to discovery. Under the California Discovery Act every party is given the right to use various methods to ask for and obtain evidence from a variety of sources, which is what "discovery" refers to. The idea being that every party should be given fair access to information and evidence. Sounds great, but the discovery process has become complicated over time. In fact, in most civil lawsuits the discovery phase of litigation is far more time-consuming and expensive than trial.

The bottom line is that you may have no idea what you're about to get yourself into when you become a party to a civil lawsuit in California. This book is meant to provide you with guidance on what you can expect in your lawsuit. Keep in mind that this is not a comprehensive description of everything you will encounter. This is intended to be a simple overview that will give you some perspective and guidance on what you can generally expect in your lawsuit. Hopefully, the information we provide here will enable you to ask more and better questions of your legal professional. Or at least it will prepare you to encounter a few things you may not have known about before.

A Walk-Through of the Litigation Process

The following chapters walk you through the litigation process in the order you are likely to encounter each phase of litigation. Let's briefly look at the phases of the litigation process this book covers.

Section 1 The Pleading Phase—we begin with the pleading phase, which is just the initial written documents that are filed with the court to initiate the lawsuit, the responding written documents that the opposing side files in response, and some of the motions that can occur during this phase. The pleading phase also discusses some basics of the legal notice that must be provided once a lawsuit is filed.

Sections 2 and 3 The Discovery Phase—next comes the discovery phase, which is the gathering of facts, witnesses, and documents—anything that could lead to evidence to be used at trial. The discovery phase discusses the techniques you can use to obtain information and evidence, the way in which parties are required to respond to discovery techniques, and some of the legal motions that parties file as part of the discovery process. Finally, the discovery section includes information about depositions and provides guidance on how you should act during your deposition.

Section 4 The Mediation and Settlement Phase—thereafter is the settlement phase, where we cover mediations and mandatory settlement conferences. In California, a majority of civil lawsuits settle before trial. You must be prepared to participate in some form of settlement procedure because nearly all parties to a lawsuit will have to do so eventually.

Section 5 Other Pretrial Concerns: Terminating Motions and Expert Witnesses—in regard to terminating motions, you should know that there are various ways in which parties try to win their lawsuit before trial. However, the methods available to do so rarely lead to success. Our due process judicial system has a strong preference for trials as opposed to court-made rulings prior to trial. Nonetheless, you should know the basics of how you or another party may file a motion with the court seeking to end the lawsuit.

Section 5 also considers expert witnesses. In today's complex world, we need specialists to testify in court to explain things to the judge or jury. Expert witnesses are unique in that they did not personally witness the facts or events related to the lawsuit. Instead, an expert's job is to review the relevant data and then give their expert opinion to the court.

Section 6 The Trial Phase—next is trial, the big show where evidence is presented and a final decision will be made. There is a lot to know about trial, as it can be quite chaotic at times. But there is an order to trial and a procedure that is used, albeit with variations by every judge. We also discuss the appeal process, so you'll know some of the basics of what occurs if a party chooses to appeal a trial court decision after trial.

No-contest clauses—finally, we discuss no-contest clauses. This section applies exclusively to trust and will cases, so if you do not have a trust or will lawsuit, then you can skip this chapter altogether.

One more note: this book is written by two California lawyers, so the information is geared toward what to expect in a California lawsuit. Other states are likely similar, but then again we do not practice in other states. Your jurisdiction may differ slightly, or substantially. Also, we practice primarily in trust and will litigation where we file lawsuits in both civil court and probate court in California. As such, we will be referring to both civil and probate matters from time to time. If you have a case that is only filed in civil court, no problem, the basics of this book will apply to you. If you have a case that is in probate court (or partly in probate court), then we have pointed out a few differences along the way. However, the main parts—such as discovery, settlements, and trial—will equally apply to you. The one caveat is the section on no-contest clauses because that is a trust and will issue only. If you are dealing with a straightforward civil case, then you can skip that section entirely.

By the end of this book you should have a better understanding of the litigation process. While you may still wonder why the process takes so long and costs so much (topics for a different book), your better understanding should allow you greater flexibility, resilience, and persistence, so you can more easily contend with the long, slow journey.

If you would like more information or have specific questions on the information provided in this book, feel free to email the authors: Keith A. Davidson (keith@aldavlaw.com) and Stewart Albertson (stewart@aldavlaw.com). You can also find more information on our law blog at www.aldavlaw.com.

In the meantime, let's delve into the litigation process, starting with the pleading phase.

Section 1

The Pleading Phase

The pleading phase refers to the process of filing the necessary documents with the court to begin a lawsuit.

Section 1 covers the process of initiating a lawsuit—from the initial pleadings to the due process of law to affirmative defenses and beyond—as well as the initial court hearing.

The pleading phase also refers to the responsive documents the defendant or respondent will file in answer to a lawsuit. We discuss the way in which parties are required to notify others that the lawsuit has been filed—called "service of process." And finally, we will discuss some of the motions that can occur during this beginning phase of litigation.

CHAPTER 1

Starting the Process

The Initial Pleading

The pleading phase refers to the process of filing the necessary documents with the court to begin a lawsuit.

A lawsuit begins with a complaint, in civil matters, or a petition, in probate matters. For purposes of this book, the term "probate" includes anything filed in probate court, including trust matters.

The purpose of a complaint or petition is the same—to put the court and the other parties on notice of the legal claims you intend to bring in your lawsuit. We call this the initial pleading because it starts the lawsuit. It sets out the legal basis that will be used for the lawsuit.

However, a complaint or petition does not require all of the facts and evidence to be included within it because it is just the starting point for the lawsuit. The court and other parties only need to know the basic claims being brought. The full evidence will come later at time of trial.

For example, let's say you are contesting a California will because you think that the person who created the will lacked capacity. In law, a person "lacking capacity" means they are unable to make decision or create a will because of a defect in their mental processing. So, you would simply allege in the initial petition that the will is invalid due to lack of capacity. You do not need to include all of the medical records, medical diagnoses, or expert opinion on capacity in your initial petition. You may not even have that information yet. Even if you did have that evidence, you would not include it because it is not necessary. All the court wants to know is what the legal claims are. Here, you are seeking to overturn a will based on lack of capacity.

The Ingredients

Think of the initial pleadings as your grocery-shopping list. It may list the ingredients that you will use for a recipe, but the shopping list only gives the ingredients, not the full recipe to make the ultimate dish. There is no need to write out the entire recipe on the shopping list because the purpose of the shopping list is to assemble the necessary ingredients at the store. Once you get home, you can then use the recipe to assemble the dish you are making. The initial pleading is the shopping list, the discovery process (where evidence is collected, see section 2) is the recipe, and the trial is the dish you are making.

Of course, that does not mean that you do not state any facts at all. You do need to state enough facts to establish your legal claims. But you do not need to state anything more than the basics.

Many people think that the judge or jury will review the initial complaint or petition, and make a decision based on the information provided in those documents. Not true. Decisions on who wins and who loses your lawsuit only come after trial (usually), and trial requires far more evidence than what is included in your initial complaint or petition. In fact, a jury will never see your initial complaint or petition, and a judge is typically not supposed to take those initials pleadings into account when deciding the facts of your case. In other words, the lawsuit will ultimately be decided based on the evidence admitted at trial, not based on the allegations contained in the initial pleadings.

Notice- Due Process of Law

Once the initial pleadings (documents) are filed, you must provide appropriate notice of your lawsuit to all interested parties—meaning every person connected to your lawsuit.

Our system of justice is based on due process of law, which simply means fairness. It would not be fair to sue someone without that person knowing about the lawsuit. As such, every legal case requires some form of notice to the "interested" parties in the lawsuit. But the type of notice required can be very different depending on the type of lawsuit you are filing.

Notice can be broken down into two broad categories: *in personam,* and *in rem* (less than a few pages into this book and already we're using Latin ... typical lawyers). *In personam* simply means you are suing a person. The person you are suing is a necessary party to the lawsuit, and a resolution cannot be achieved without the court having personal jurisdiction over that person.

Procedurally, a court obtains personal jurisdiction over a person once the person is personally served with a summons and copy of the legal complaint. In other words, you must be personally handed a summons (which is just a piece of paper ordering you to appear and answer the lawsuit) and a copy of the complaint BEFORE the lawsuit can begin. Ever wonder why some people try to evade being given a summons? This is why. The process of serving a person with a summons and complaint is called "service of process"—meaning service of due process on the individual.

In rem is a bit different because that involves lawsuits over property, not people. For example, a lawsuit involving a trust contest involves the ultimate distribution of property. The court can resolve the issue by simply ordering the trust assets to be distributed to certain people. As such, no one person needs to be a party to the lawsuit for the court to resolve the case. Interested parties can join the case and argue their side if they choose to do so, but it is not necessary to resolve the case.

Compare this to a personal injury lawsuit where the court may enter a judgment requiring one person to pay money to another person. When a person is required to pay money, you must have personal jurisdiction. When a fund of money or property, like a trust or will, is the subject of the lawsuit, then personal jurisdiction is not required because no one person is paying anything. Instead, the trust or estate fund is transferring assets out to people.

For *in rem* cases, the only notice you typically need is by mail to the persons interested in the trust fund or estate. It is up to each person whether they want to appear or not. Personal service is, therefore, not required.

If this is all a bit too confusing, don't worry about it. All you need to know is that your lawsuit will not begin until the proper type of notice has been given. This is an important first step to any lawsuit.

Verified Pleadings– Telling the Truth, the Whole Truth

There are two ways to allege facts in a complaint or petition: verified or unverified. Verified simply means that a party to the lawsuit has signed an oath under penalty of perjury that the facts contained in the initial pleadings are true. Here is a sample verification:

Verification

I, Bob Client, am the Petitioner in the above-entitled proceeding. I read the foregoing document and know its contents. The facts stated in the foregoing document are true based on my own knowledge, except as to those matters stated on information and belief, and as to those matters I believe them to be true.

I declare under penalty of perjury under the laws of the State of California that the foregoing is true and correct and that this verification was executed on _____, 2018 at Los Angeles, California.

If a party knowingly states false facts in a document, but then verifies that document, then the party can be prosecuted for perjury. This verification is the same as the oath administered to every witness during trial. You've seen the television shows and movies where a witness takes the stand, holds up their right hand, and repeats the saying that they "promise to tell the truth, the whole truth," etc.? A verification is the same thing.

Some pleadings must be verified while others can be verified at the option of the party filing the document. So, sometimes verification is required, and other times, when it's not required, a party may choose to do it anyway. In civil lawsuits, the initial complaint need not be verified (usually— some exceptions apply). But a party may choose to file a "verified complaint," which is the same complaint as it would otherwise be without verification; it just has the verification language mentioned above at the end of it. In probate lawsuits, nearly all pleadings must be verified. When a party verifies their initial pleadings, then the responding parties are required to also file verified answers or responses.

Answering the Pleadings

Once your initial pleadings are filed, and proper notice has been provided, then the opposing parties to the lawsuit have the right, and sometimes the obligation, to file an answer (or objection or response—all the same thing, but it varies depending on the type of lawsuit involved). The answer is simply the starting response to the initial lawsuit. Answers come in many different forms. Just as with the initial complaint or petition, an answer need not include all the facts and evidence but rather, just the basics to articulate the legal basis for the answer.

If the initial complaint was unverified—meaning it was not signed under penalty of perjury—then the responding party can file a general denial. A "general denial" refers to a legal solutions form document. A general denial simply states that the party responding to the lawsuit denies all given allegations.

By the way, most of the time lawyers prefer not to verify complaints or answers if they are not required to do so. The reason for this is that we know so little of the facts at the outset of a lawsuit. Most lawsuits are filed based solely from a client's recollections or belief of events. Those beliefs and recollections can change, or be proven untrue, once evidence is gathered during the discovery process. Most lawyers do not want to lock in their client's facts without first being able to corroborate those facts with other evidence.

For example, a client might tell us that their parent was diagnosed with dementia. But after we subpoena the parent's medical records we find no support for that fact—there is no reference to a dementia diagnosis in the medical records. Was the client lying to us? No, not in most cases. Either the client was mistaken, or the client heard the doctor mention dementia, but that diagnosis was never finalized or recorded in the medical records. It doesn't matter to us which is the case, we just don't want the client saying one thing, and then other evidence making the client appear to be wrong, or worse yet, deceitful. This is why lawyers prefer not to verify complaints or answers if it isn't required.

PLD-050

ATTORNEY OR PARTY WITHOUT ATTORNEY *(Name, State Bar number, and address):*	FOR COURT USE ONLY

TELEPHONE NO.:   FAX NO. *(Optional)*:

E-MAIL ADDRESS *(Optional)*:

ATTORNEY FOR *(Name)*:

SUPERIOR COURT OF CALIFORNIA, COUNTY OF

    STREET ADDRESS:

    MAILING ADDRESS:

    CITY AND ZIP CODE:

    BRANCH NAME:

PLAINTIFF/PETITIONER:

DEFENDANT/RESPONDENT:

GENERAL DENIAL	CASE NUMBER:

If you want to file a general denial, you MUST use this form if the amount asked for in the complaint or the value of the property involved is $1,000 or less.

You MAY use this form for a general denial if:

    1. The complaint is not verified; *or*

    2. The complaint is verified and the case is a limited civil case (the amount in controversy is $25,000 or less), BUT NOT if the complaint involves a claim for more than $1,000 that has been assigned to a third party for collection.

(See Code of Civil Procedure sections 85–86, 90–100, 431.30, and 431.40.)

1. DEFENDANT *(name):*

    generally denies each and every allegation of plaintiff's complaint.

2. ☐   DEFENDANT states the following FACTS as separate affirmative defenses to plaintiff's complaint *(attach additional pages if necessary):*

Date:

▶

(TYPE OR PRINT NAME)   (SIGNATURE OF DEFENDANT OR ATTORNEY)

If you have a claim for damages or other relief against the plaintiff, the law may require you to state your claim in a special pleading called a cross-complaint or you may lose your right to bring the claim. (See Code of Civil Procedure sections 426.10–426.40.)

The original of this *General Denial* must be filed with the clerk of this court with proof that a copy was served on each plaintiff's attorney and on each plaintiff not represented by an attorney. There are two main ways to serve this *General Denial*: by personal delivery or by mail. It may be served by anyone at least 18 years of age EXCEPT you or any other party to this legal action. Be sure that whoever serves the *General Denial* fills out and signs a proof of service. You may use the applicable Judicial Council form (such as form POS-020, POS-030, or POS-040) for the proof of service.

Page 1 of 1

Form Adopted for Mandatory Use Judicial Council of California PLD-050 [Rev. January 1, 2009]	GENERAL DENIAL	Code of Civil Procedure, §§ 431.30, 431.40 www.courtinfo.ca.gov American LegalNet, Inc. www.FormsWorkflow.com

Initial petitions in probate court are different from civil court because all probate petitions must be verified. As such, the response must be a bit more involved than civil court responses where a general denial can be used. However, a responding party can simply go through the paragraphs of the initial petition and either admit or deny each paragraph.

For example, a petition might state in paragraph one "Bob Smith was the father of Randy Smith and Rachel Smith." In response, if those facts were accurate, you would state, "Responding party admits the facts stated in paragraph one of the petition." In paragraph two, the petition party states, "Bob Smith lacks capacity." In response, if you disagreed, you would state, "Responding party denies the facts stated in paragraph two of the petition." You can even admit some of the facts in a paragraph, but deny the rest by stating, "Responding party admits that Bob Smith was diagnosed with dementia but denies the remainder of the paragraph." Whatever the case may be, you are simply establishing the parts of the petition you agree with (admit) and the parts you disagree with (deny).

1 | **A.**   **Specific Denials**

2 | 1.   As to paragraph 1, Respondent admits that Sophie worked as a teacher.

3 | Respondent denies the remainder of paragraph 1.

4 | 2.   As to paragraph 2, Respondent denies each and every allegation.

5 | 3.   As to paragraph 3, Respondent denies that he verbally harassed Sophie.

6 | Respondent lacks sufficient knowledge or information to form a belief as to the truth of

7 | the remaining allegations contained therein and, on that basis, denies said allegations.

8 | 4.   As to paragraph 4, Respondent denies each and every allegation.

9 | 5.   As to paragraph 5, Respondent admits that Sophie was diagnosed with

10 | breast cancer. Respondent lacks sufficient knowledge or information to form a belief as

11 | to the truth of the remaining allegations contained therein and, on that basis, denies said

12 | allegations.

13 | 6.   As to paragraph 6, Respondent admits that Sophie's cancer progressed until

14 | her death. Respondent lacks sufficient knowledge or information to form a belief as to

15 | the truth of the remaining allegations contained therein and, on that basis, denies said

16 | allegations.

17 | 7.   As to paragraph 7, Respondent denies he was aware that Sophie executed a

18 | Trust on April 18, 2017.

19 | 8.   As to paragraph 8, Respondent denies, generally and specifically, each and

20 | every allegation.

21 | **B.**   **Prayer for Relief**

22 | WHEREFORE, Respondent prays for orders as follows:

23 | 1.   The Petition is denied in its entirety, and that the court denies all relief

24 | requested;

25 | 2.   Awards Respondent his reasonable attorney fees incurred to defend this

26 | Petition;

27 | 3.   Awards Respondent his cost of suits incurred herein; and

28 | 4.   Grants such other and further orders as the court deems just and proper.

2

Respondent Samuel Erickson's Objection and Response to Petition, et al.

This same format would be used for civil complaints that are verified. If you are responding to the initial complaint another party filed, you might wonder whether you can include additional facts in your response. Yes, you can state any factual allegations you like in your response. But you need not state all the facts and evidence. Just as with the initial pleadings, the response is a notice pleading—meaning it puts the parties on notice of the legal basis for your response.

There are times when you may not want to state too much in your initial pleadings. For example, if you don't know all the facts and evidence yet, then you can't state that information. Also, you may think you know the facts, but you have no evidence to support the facts yet. As a result, those facts may change, or later found evidence may prove the factual allegations untrue. If you are signing a verified response (remember, signed under penalty of perjury), then you may have a problem if facts are later proved untrue. To safeguard yourself from future evidence being discovered, it may be best to either (1) state less facts rather than more, and (2) state some facts on "information and belief."

Leave it to lawyers to find a way out of verified pleadings. Stating a factual allegation on "information and belief" means you think the fact may be true, but you are basing it solely on the information and belief you have at the time you sign the document. In other words, this is not an absolute fact yet. You cannot base all your factual allegations on information and belief, but anytime you have a fact that is not supported yet by evidence, you should consider protecting yourself with an allegation based on "information and belief."

The bottom line for initial pleadings and responding to them: say enough, but not too much.

Affirmative Defenses

There is another aspect to answering/responding to a complaint or petition: affirmative defenses. An affirmative defense is a concession that you committed the act, but you provide evidence that justifies or excuses what you did, and this evidence should overcome the claim. There is a difference between denying allegations made in a complaint and asserting your own reasons for why you (as the responding party) should not be held liable. Basically, think of it as supplying extra evidence that could serve as a legitimate excuse.

The best example of an affirmative defense is a statute of limitations. The plaintiff may say you are liable to pay damages for a car crash. As a defendant, you can deny that claim. However, you can also assert that the claim is barred by the statute of limitations if the plaintiff filed the lawsuit too late. Asserting the statute of limitations as a defense to your lawsuit is an affirmative defense. It references something that was not stated in the initial complaint but rather was an extra issue asserted by you in your answer that should excuse you.

There are many different types of affirmative defenses, and you have to state them at the time you respond or they could be waived. At times, a party may state over twenty affirmative defenses in their pleadings—it can get a bit voluminous. That does not mean that every affirmative defense is supported by facts. Rather, it usually is the sign of an overprotective attorney.

Side Bar on Criminal Charges

When you bring your lawsuit, whether it be in civil or probate court, your rights are limited to what the law allows you to bring. In other words, you are not allowed to sue for things for which the law does not provide you with a legal right to sue.

Often, clients will want to know if something the other party did was criminal, and they may want to bring criminal charges against the other party. As a civil litigant (which you are in a civil lawsuit) you have no right to bring criminal charges. In fact, no private citizen has the right to bring criminal charges against another person or entity. Only governmental agencies can file and prosecute criminal charges.

If you think something is criminal, your first step is to report the alleged crime to law enforcement—the police, sheriff, FBI, etc. Law enforcement will investigate the crime and then refer the matter to the district attorney's office to determine whether criminal charges will be filed.

You have no role in this process other than reporting the crime to law enforcement. Just be forewarned that neither you, nor your lawyer, has the ability to file criminal charges in court.

Attacking the Initial Pleadings

"This lawsuit is full of lies. Can't the judge just throw it out?" In a word—no. The court does not have the power to throw out a lawsuit because it is "full of lies." In fact, pleadings are meant to be inaccurate. Can you believe that?

In our judicial system, pleadings are meant to put the other side on notice about the legal claims being brought. Notice pleadings must state enough facts to establish a legal claim, but no more than that. In the legal world, we call the "facts" stated in the pleadings "allegations." In other words, the allegations are not yet proven to be true. Allegations are just allegations—assertions that may or may not be true. These allegations provide the initial facts that will be used to start the lawsuit.

That's not to say you can intentionally lie in a court pleading, especially in probate court pleadings where the petition must be verified under penalty of perjury. Intentional lies will eventually be discovered. But many pleadings are made "on information and belief," meaning the party thinks the facts are accurate, but the party is not making an absolute statement that the facts are true. This is a bit like when you ask your child, "Did you take out the trash?" and they answer, "I think I did," which means they probably didn't. It may sound a bit sketchy, but allegations made on information and belief are sufficient to get the lawsuit started. Welcome to litigation.

Allegations do have a role in the lawsuit. They provide the opening act of your lawsuit, the introductory section, the movie trailer. You must state enough facts to legally support the claims you are making in your lawsuit. But you need not state every fact that the judge or jury will ultimately hear or see at trial. Lawyers want to ensure they state enough facts to avoid the lawsuit being attacked by a demurrer or motion to strike (more on that below), but lawyers are not expected to state all relevant facts. Under the law, we refer to the initial pleadings as "notice pleadings" that put all people connected to the lawsuit on notice of what legal claims are being made and the basic facts that support those claims.

The allegations in a legal complaint will never be seen by the jury. Instead, at time of trial the jury sees only admissible evidence. Then the jury will decide what is true and what is untrue. As such, the court has no power to decide the truthfulness of allegations at the beginning of a case. Again, this is a requirement of due process: allowing each party a fair chance to present evidence in front of the trier-of-fact (judge or jury, depending on the type of case). Until the evidentiary trial takes place, no decision can be made on the truthfulness, or falsity, of the allegations.

However, in some cases a party may decide to attack the initial pleadings filed. This can only be done for very limited purposes. For example, a petition must state certain fundamental elements to be properly pleaded. If a certain element is missing, it can be attacked either by a "demurrer" or "motion to strike." In most cases, even if a demurrer or motion to strike is successful, the opposing party will have the right to amend their pleadings to correct any deficiencies.

Parties are not allowed to use demurrers and motions to strike to question the truthfulness of the allegations in a complaint. In fact, the law requires that allegations contained in a complaint be assumed as true for purposes of deciding a demurrer or motion to strike.

The demurrer or motion to strike only challenges the technical aspects of a pleading. It questions whether sufficient allegations were made to support the elements for a given cause of action. For example, if a person sues you for breach of contract, then they need to allege that they had a contract with you. If the lawsuit fails to state that in the allegations, then you could file a demurrer and challenge the complaint. Unfortunately, in most cases even if you win the demurrer, the court will give the plaintiff a chance to amend their complaint. The plaintiff can simply file an amended complaint and state that there was a contract—problem solved.

For this reason, most demurrers and motions to strike are not worth bringing. The costs of bringing a demurrer or motion to strike can be substantial, and the results can be of little value. There are some exceptions, such as a lawsuit brought after the statute of limitations expires. In this case, a demurrer may end a case for good. But those situations are rare.

The other reason you may find yourself dealing with a demurrer or motion to strike filed by the opposing party is to cause you to have to work and spend money. Many litigants will bring baseless motions under the belief that it wears down the opposing party—and sometimes it does just that.

Once you get past any attacks on the pleading, you can then proceed to the next step, the initial court hearing.

CHAPTER 2

The Initial Court Hearing

Probate Court Cases

In California Probate Court, every petition filed receives a hearing date. The initial hearing date is usually scheduled from thirty to sixty days after the petition is filed. Very little happens at the initial hearing date set by the court.

The initial hearing date is NOT a trial date. In fact, nothing is usually decided. The date is simply the first opportunity for the court to review the petition and determine if anyone is going to object to the petition. The court will also determine if proper notice was given on the petition because the court cannot take action until proper notice is given. In California, proper notice for matters dealing with wills is fifteen days before the hearing date; for matters dealing with trusts it's thirty days before the hearing date. If the court sees a problem with the notice, then the hearing will be continued for proper notice to be provided to all interested parties.

Under California law, anyone wanting to object to the petition can appear at the initial hearing and tell the judge verbally that they object to it. The court will then order that the objections be made in writing by a certain date after the hearing date. Alternatively, written objections can be filed before the initial hearing date. Either way, the hearing date will be continued to allow the parties to engage in discovery.

If you have a lawyer, then you typically do not need to appear at the initial court hearing because your lawyer will appear on your behalf. If you do not have a lawyer, then you should appear at the initial hearing, especially if you object to the petition. Of course, you always have the right to attend every court hearing in your matter even if you have a lawyer representing you. There are times when your appearance in court will be mandatory, such as during a mandatory settlement conference or at trial. Be sure you are able and willing to travel to court if you decide to become a party to a probate petition because there are times when your appearance is mandatory.

Civil Lawsuit: All Non-Probate Court Matters

Civil cases work very differently from probate cases. In civil lawsuits, the plaintiff is expected to file proof of service of process with the court before any court hearings take place. In fact, most courts will dismiss a lawsuit on their own if proper proof of service is not filed within a reasonable time. Proof of service refers to a written declaration signed by the person who handed the lawsuit paperwork to the defendant. In other words, the declaration gives proof to the court that proper personal service was accomplished by someone personally delivering the documents to the defendant. The person who hands people lawsuit documents is referred to as a process server. You can think of a process server as similar to a server at a restaurant, except the item they serve is far less delicious.

To start a civil lawsuit, the plaintiff is required to personally serve the defendant(s) with a copy of the complaint and summons. The complaint is just the legal term for the initial filing that starts the lawsuit and cites the grounds for the lawsuit. A summons is a single piece of paper issued by the clerk of the court ordering the defendant(s) to appear and answer the lawsuit.

SUM-100

SUMMONS
(CITACION JUDICIAL)

NOTICE TO DEFENDANT:
(AVISO AL DEMANDADO):

YOU ARE BEING SUED BY PLAINTIFF:
(LO ESTÁ DEMANDANDO EL DEMANDANTE):

FOR COURT USE ONLY
(SOLO PARA USO DE LA CORTE)

NOTICE! You have been sued. The court may decide against you without your being heard unless you respond within 30 days. Read the information below.

You have 30 CALENDAR DAYS after this summons and legal papers are served on you to file a written response at this court and have a copy served on the plaintiff. A letter or phone call will not protect you. Your written response must be in proper legal form if you want the court to hear your case. There may be a court form that you can use for your response. You can find these court forms and more information at the California Courts Online Self-Help Center (www.courtinfo.ca.gov/selfhelp), your county law library, or the courthouse nearest you. If you cannot pay the filing fee, ask the court clerk for a fee waiver form. If you do not file your response on time, you may lose the case by default, and your wages, money, and property may be taken without further warning from the court.

There are other legal requirements. You may want to call an attorney right away. If you do not know an attorney, you may want to call an attorney referral service. If you cannot afford an attorney, you may be eligible for free legal services from a nonprofit legal services program. You can locate these nonprofit groups at the California Legal Services Web site (www.lawhelpcalifornia.org), the California Courts Online Self-Help Center (www.courtinfo.ca.gov/selfhelp), or by contacting your local court or county bar association. NOTE: The court has a statutory lien for waived fees and costs on any settlement or arbitration award of $10,000 or more in a civil case. The court's lien must be paid before the court will dismiss the case.

¡AVISO! Lo han demandado. Si no responde dentro de 30 días, la corte puede decidir en su contra sin escuchar su versión. Lea la información a continuación.

Tiene 30 DÍAS DE CALENDARIO después de que le entreguen esta citación y papeles legales para presentar una respuesta por escrito en esta corte y hacer que se entregue una copia al demandante. Una carta o una llamada telefónica no lo protegen. Su respuesta por escrito tiene que estar en formato legal correcto si desea que procesen su caso en la corte. Es posible que haya un formulario que usted pueda usar para su respuesta. Puede encontrar estos formularios de la corte y más información en el Centro de Ayuda de las Cortes de California (www.sucorte.ca.gov), en la biblioteca de leyes de su condado o en la corte que le quede más cerca. Si no puede pagar la cuota de presentación, pida al secretario de la corte que le dé un formulario de exención de pago de cuotas. Si no presenta su respuesta a tiempo, puede perder el caso por incumplimiento y la corte le podrá quitar su sueldo, dinero y bienes sin más advertencia.

Hay otros requisitos legales. Es recomendable que llame a un abogado inmediatamente. Si no conoce a un abogado, puede llamar a un servicio de remisión a abogados. Si no puede pagar a un abogado, es posible que cumpla con los requisitos para obtener servicios legales gratuitos de un programa de servicios legales sin fines de lucro. Puede encontrar estos grupos sin fines de lucro en el sitio web de California Legal Services, (www.lawhelpcalifornia.org), en el Centro de Ayuda de las Cortes de California, (www.sucorte.ca.gov) o poniéndose en contacto con la corte o el colegio de abogados locales. AVISO: Por ley, la corte tiene derecho a reclamar las cuotas y los costos exentos por imponer un gravamen sobre cualquier recuperación de $10,000 o más de valor recibida mediante un acuerdo o una concesión de arbitraje en un caso de derecho civil. Tiene que pagar el gravamen de la corte antes de que la corte pueda desechar el caso.

The name and address of the court is:
(El nombre y dirección de la corte es):

CASE NUMBER:
(Número del Caso):

The name, address, and telephone number of plaintiff's attorney, or plaintiff without an attorney, is:
(El nombre, la dirección y el número de teléfono del abogado del demandante, o del demandante que no tiene abogado, es):

DATE: _____ Clerk, by _____, Deputy
(Fecha) *(Secretario)* *(Adjunto)*

(For proof of service of this summons, use Proof of Service of Summons (form POS-010).)
(Para prueba de entrega de esta citatión use el formulario Proof of Service of Summons, (POS-010)).

NOTICE TO THE PERSON SERVED: You are served
[SEAL]
1. ☐ as an individual defendant.
2. ☐ as the person sued under the fictitious name of *(specify)*:
3. ☐ on behalf of *(specify)*:
   under: ☐ CCP 416.10 (corporation)   ☐ CCP 416.60 (minor)
          ☐ CCP 416.20 (defunct corporation) ☐ CCP 416.70 (conservatee)
          ☐ CCP 416.40 (association or partnership) ☐ CCP 416.90 (authorized person)
          ☐ other *(specify)*:
4. ☐ by personal delivery on *(date)*:

Page 1 of 1

Form Adopted for Mandatory Use
Judicial Council of California
SUM-100 [Rev. July 1, 2009]

SUMMONS

Code of Civil Procedure §§ 412.20, 465
www.courtinfo.ca.gov

In a civil lawsuit, the defendant(s) is required to file an answer within thirty days of being served with a complaint. If an answer is not filed, then the plaintiff has the right to ask the court to enter a default and get a default judgment against the defendant. A "default" simply means the defendant failed to file an answer within thirty days. In other words, if the defendant does not answer, the defendant loses the lawsuit and may be obligated to pay money to the plaintiff. For this reason, it is important that you hire a lawyer immediately if ever you are served with a civil lawsuit.

Typically, the first hearing date in a civil lawsuit is the case management conference hearing. A case management conference is usually scheduled for six months after the initial complaint is filed. Again, this is NOT the trial date, it is just the first chance the court has to check in with the parties and determine how much time they will need for the discovery process. You typically do not need to appear at a case management conference hearing because your lawyer will appear on your behalf. Plus, not much occurs at these hearings. Of course, you are always welcome to attend every court hearing in your matter.

Prior to the case management conference, you are required to file a case management statement. And you are also required to "meet and confer" with the opposing party when preparing your case management statement. The purpose for the statement is to inform the court on what has transpired so far in your case. What are the core factual disputes? Have you conducted discovery, and if so, what remains to be completed? Have you considered going to mediation or a mandatory settlement conference?

In other words, the court wants to know the status of your case. And the court wants you to discuss these important status issues with the opposing party, so you can coordinate

YOUR LAWSUIT • 35

some of the procedural issues your case will encounter. For example, will your case have a judge or jury trial? How many days of trial do you anticipate having? The court will ultimately decide all those procedural issues, but it wants your input through the case management statement. For that reason, you should take the case management statement seriously and spend some time preparing it before filing.

At times the first court hearing in a civil case will be on a demurrer or motion to strike if a defendant chooses to attack the pleadings early on in the case. As with any motion hearing, the court will simply review the written motions beforehand and then make a rule, either in court in front of the parties, or it will take the matter under submission and rule on the motion later.

Section- 1 Brief

As you can see, starting a lawsuit is no easy task. There are many strategies to consider, documents to prepare, and procedural hoops to clear before your lawsuit is properly filed and ready to be addressed by the court. Patience is crucial. The opening act of your lawsuit should not be rushed as it sets the tone for the work that is to come, such as, locating evidence to support your legal claims. And that brings us to the world of discovery, our next section.

Section 2

The Discovery Phase: Written Discovery

D iscovery is the processes by which parties to a lawsuit attempt to obtain information, documents, statements, and any other relevant facts pertaining to the case, some of which will be used as evidence at trial.

You can think of discovery in two broad categories (1) written discovery, which is the focus of this section, and (2) depositions, the focus of section 3.

Let's delve into written discovery.

CHAPTER 3

Written Discovery- Document Demand

Written discovery begins with the demand of documents. Document demands are served on opposing parties and require them to produce relevant documents pertaining to the lawsuit that are in their possession or control. Document demands can only be served on parties to the lawsuit. As mentioned already, parties refer to people or entities that have either been named in a lawsuit or have voluntarily joined it. If you want to obtain documents from a non-party, then you must use the subpoena process described later in this section.

The document demand is more accurately called an inspection demand because you can use this process to review and inspect anything that is relevant to the lawsuit. For example, you could issue an inspection demand to look at an original document, a piece of equipment, or a location. That does not happen too often in most lawsuits, but the process is there if you need it.

Making a Document Demand

More commonly, this process is used to demand copies of documents from the opposing party. When asking for documents using a document demand, it is your burden to describe the category of documents you are requesting. In other words, the opposing party is not obligated to hand over all relevant documents without you asking for them. Instead, you must state in a written document demand the types of documents you want to see.

For example, let's consider a "capacity case." As mentioned already, in law, a person without "capacity" means they are unable to make decision or create a will because of a defect in their mental processing. In a capacity case, you would need to see medical records for someone who dies to determine if they lack capacity prior to their death. Accordingly, you would ask the opposing party to "produce all medical records for Mr. John Smith covering the dates from January 1, 2019 to December 31, 2019." This becomes a category of documents that the opposing party must produce to you if they have the documents.

Your obligation in creating and serving a document demand is to state a clear category of documents that the opposing party can understand and produce to you. You want your requests to be broad enough to include all relevant documents needed for your lawsuit, but not too broad so as to draw an objection from the opposing party. For instance, if I were to ask for all medical documents for Mr. Smith from his birth to his death, that would be too broad in most cases.

Most of the time it is easy enough to state the category of documents you seek. But you do need to be careful in how you describe those documents to avoid drawing any objections. The goal is to obtain relevant evidence.

Responding to a Document Demand

When you serve a document demand on an opponent, there are two things they must give you in return. First, they must provide a written response to your document demand that states whether they will produce the documents or not. If a party states that they will not produce the documents, then they must state why they are not producing them.

For example, if the documents are protected by the attorney-client privilege because they are letters between the party and their lawyer, then they must state that objection. If they simply have no documents that fit your request, then they must tell you that and tell you why they don't have the documents—either the documents never existed, they were lost, or they were destroyed.

Second, the opposing party must provide you with the documents that they agreed to produce. If you just receive a response and no documents, then the opposing party has not finished their obligations under the Discovery Act. It is important that you receive both the response and the documents from the opposing party.

Once a document demand is served on an opposing party, that party has thirty days in which to respond. They may ask you (or your lawyer) for an extension of time in which to respond. The parties (or their lawyers) can agree to extend these deadlines, and they often are extended. The primary reason to grant an extension is that the court does not look kindly on refusals to grant reasonable extensions. As such, the document demand may not be responded to until forty-five to sixty days after it is served. The goal is to obtain evidence, even if it does not arrive as quickly as you like.

Once a response is received it may be insufficient. It may contain baseless objections or refuse to provide all relevant documents. California law requires that the parties attempt to "meet and confer" on such disputes, meaning that you send a letter to the opposing party outlining your problems with their response (you can talk by phone or in person too, but a letter is the customary option). The opposing party usually agrees to provide a supplemental response within a set period of time.

Once the supplemental response is received, it may still be insufficient. Sometimes a response is insufficient because the other party is incompetent or playing games, but sometimes it's the result of a difference of opinion between the lawyers as to what is sufficient. Intelligent minds can disagree on what is required to be produced, and what is not. If you believe the responses are insufficient, another "meet and confer" is required. If the opposition refuses to supplement their response again, then you must file a motion with the court and ask the court to force the opposition to respond. See the discussion of discovery motions listed below.

Note that document demands may only be served on parties to the lawsuit. They are not allowed for third-party witnesses, such as banks, brokerage firms, insurance companies, healthcare providers, or any other individuals who are not parties to the lawsuit. To obtain documents from third parties requires that you issue a subpoena, the topic addressed in the next chapter.

CHAPTER 4

Written Discovery-
Subpoenas

Subpoenas are demands made to third-party witnesses (also referred to as non-party witnesses) requiring them to hand over relevant documents or other information. Subpoenas are also used to take the deposition of non-party witnesses. When bank records or medical records are required, you must issue a subpoena to the entity that has the records.

SUBP-010

ATTORNEY OR PARTY WITHOUT ATTORNEY *(Name, State Bar number, and address)*:

FOR COURT USE ONLY

TELEPHONE NO.: FAX NO.:
E-MAIL ADDRESS:
ATTORNEY FOR *(Name)*:

SUPERIOR COURT OF CALIFORNIA, COUNTY OF
STREET ADDRESS:
MAILING ADDRESS:
CITY AND ZIP CODE:
BRANCH NAME:

PLAINTIFF/PETITIONER:

DEFENDANT/RESPONDENT:

DEPOSITION SUBPOENA
FOR PRODUCTION OF BUSINESS RECORDS

CASE NUMBER:

THE PEOPLE OF THE STATE OF CALIFORNIA, TO *(name, address, and telephone number of deponent, if known)*:

1. YOU ARE ORDERED TO PRODUCE THE BUSINESS RECORDS described in item 3, as follows:

To *(name of deposition officer)*:
On *(date)*: At *(time)*:
Location *(address)*:
 Do not release the requested records to the deposition officer prior to the date and time stated above.

 a. ☐ by delivering a true, legible, and durable **copy** of the business records described in item 3, enclosed in a sealed inner wrapper with the title and number of the action, name of witness, and date of subpoena clearly written on it. The inner wrapper shall then be enclosed in an outer envelope or wrapper, sealed, and mailed to the deposition officer at the address in item 1.

 b. ☐ by delivering a true, legible, and durable **copy** of the business records described in item 3 to the deposition officer at the witness's address, on receipt of payment in cash or by check of the reasonable costs of preparing the copy, as determined under Evidence Code section 1563(b).

 c. ☐ by making the **original** business records described in item 3 available for inspection at your business address by the attorney's representative and permitting **copying** at your business address under reasonable conditions during normal business hours.

2. *The records are to be produced by the date and time shown in item 1 (but not sooner than 20 days after the issuance of the deposition subpoena, or 15 days after service, whichever date is later). Reasonable costs of locating records, making them available or copying them, and postage, if any, are recoverable as set forth in Evidence Code section 1563(b). The records shall be accompanied by an affidavit of the custodian or other qualified witness pursuant to Evidence Code section 1561.*

3. The records to be produced are described as follows *(if electronically stored information is demanded, the form or forms in which each type of information is to be produced may be specified)*:

 ☐ Continued on Attachment 3.

4. IF YOU HAVE BEEN SERVED WITH THIS SUBPOENA AS A CUSTODIAN OF CONSUMER OR EMPLOYEE RECORDS UNDER CODE OF CIVIL PROCEDURE SECTION 1985.3 OR 1985.6 AND A MOTION TO QUASH OR AN OBJECTION HAS BEEN SERVED ON YOU, A COURT ORDER OR AGREEMENT OF THE PARTIES, WITNESSES, AND CONSUMER OR EMPLOYEE AFFECTED MUST BE OBTAINED BEFORE YOU ARE REQUIRED TO PRODUCE CONSUMER OR EMPLOYEE RECORDS.

DISOBEDIENCE OF THIS SUBPOENA MAY BE PUNISHED AS CONTEMPT BY THIS COURT. YOU WILL ALSO BE LIABLE FOR THE SUM OF FIVE HUNDRED DOLLARS AND ALL DAMAGES RESULTING FROM YOUR FAILURE TO OBEY.

Date issued:

▶

(TYPE OR PRINT NAME) (SIGNATURE OF PERSON ISSUING SUBPOENA)

(TITLE)

(Proof of service on reverse) Page 1 of 2

Form Adopted for Mandatory Use
Judicial Council of California
SUBP-010 [Rev. January 1, 2012]

DEPOSITION SUBPOENA FOR PRODUCTION
OF BUSINESS RECORDS

Code of Civil Procedure, §§ 2020.410–2020.440;
Government Code, § 68097.1
www.courts.ca.gov

Obtaining documents through subpoenas is time-consuming. For example, when requesting bank records, you are required to give a "Consumer's Notice" to everyone whose name is associated with the bank account. Only after each person associated with a given bank account is given time to voice an objection can you serve the subpoena on the bank. The bank then has twenty days in which to comply and produce the documents, but they rarely meet this deadline. Thus, it can take from thirty to sixty to ninety days in some cases to receive documents from a bank or any other third-party witness, such as an insurance company or medical provider. And if the bank is located outside California (meaning they do not do business in California), then the process can take twice as long. Persistence pays dividends in obtaining documents from banks and other financial institutions. The goal is to retrieve the documents no matter how long it may take.

There are companies that assist with issuing subpoenas and obtaining documents from third-party witnesses. These companies also will serve as the "deposition officer," meaning they receive the documents from the third-party witness and make them available to all parties in your lawsuit. Of course, each party must pay for copies of the documents, but that is up to each party to do, or not do, on their own. The person who issues the subpoena must also pay the company who is being asked to produce the documents. That company will want to be paid for their time and the copy costs for assembling and providing the documents to you or your deposition officer. These costs add up if you are issuing subpoenas to many different companies.

Subpoenas are an effective way to obtain relevant documents from people and companies that are not part of your lawsuit. But you must issue your subpoenas as early as possible because it takes time to process and then receive documents back from third-party witnesses. And there is a cost to issuing subpoenas and receiving documents because you must pay for the documents you receive. As such, you want to be judicious when issuing subpoenas to ensure you spend your money wisely.

So far we have only discussed how to obtain documents from other people. You also have the right to ask written questions of other parties to the lawsuit, which brings us to interrogatories.

CHAPTER 5

Written Discovery- Interrogatories

nterrogatories are just written questions asked of the opposing parties. There are two types of interrogatories—
form interrogatories (asking a set of pre-printed questions) and special interrogatories (attorney-drafted questions).

Form interrogatories are easy to issue because the California Judicial Council has issued forms you can use for this purpose. You simply mark the box next to each question you
want to ask and then serve the form to the opposing party.
The benefit of form interrogatories is that they are easy to
use. The detriment is that the questions are very general and
generic.

DISC-001

ATTORNEY OR PARTY WITHOUT ATTORNEY *(Name, State Bar number, and address)*:

TELEPHONE NO.:
FAX NO. *(Optional)*:
E-MAIL ADDRESS *(Optional)*:
ATTORNEY FOR *(Name)*:

SUPERIOR COURT OF CALIFORNIA, COUNTY OF

SHORT TITLE OF CASE:

FORM INTERROGATORIES—GENERAL

Asking Party:

Answering Party:
Set No.:

CASE NUMBER

Sec. 1. Instructions to All Parties
(a) Interrogatories are written questions prepared by a party to an action that are sent to any other party in the action to be answered under oath. The interrogatories below are form interrogatories approved for use in civil cases.

(b) For time limitations, requirements for service on other parties, and other details, see Code of Civil Procedure sections 2030.010–2030.410 and the cases construing those sections.

(c) These form interrogatories do not change existing law relating to interrogatories nor do they affect an answering party's right to assert any privilege or make any objection.

Sec. 2. Instructions to the Asking Party
(a) These interrogatories are designed for optional use by parties in unlimited civil cases where the amount demanded exceeds $25,000. Separate interrogatories, Form Interrogatories—Limited Civil Cases (Economic Litigation) (form DISC-004), which have no subparts, are designed for use in limited civil cases where the amount demanded is $25,000 or less; however, those interrogatories may also be used in unlimited civil cases.

(b) Check the box next to each interrogatory that you want the answering party to answer. Use care in choosing those interrogatories that are applicable to the case.

(c) You may insert your own definition of INCIDENT in Section 4, but only where the action arises from a course of conduct or a series of events occurring over a period of time.

(d) The interrogatories in section 16.0, Defendant's Contentions–Personal Injury, should not be used until the defendant has had a reasonable opportunity to conduct an investigation or discovery of plaintiff's injuries and damages.

(e) Additional interrogatories may be attached.

Sec. 3. Instructions to the Answering Party
(a) An answer or other appropriate response must be given to each interrogatory checked by the asking party.

(b) As a general rule, within 30 days after you are served with these interrogatories, you must serve your responses on the asking party and serve copies of your responses on all other parties to the action who have appeared. See Code of Civil Procedure sections 2030.260–2030.270 for details.

(c) Each answer must be as complete and straightforward as the information reasonably available to you, including the information possessed by your attorneys or agents, permits. If an interrogatory cannot be answered completely, answer it to the extent possible.

(d) If you do not have enough personal knowledge to fully answer an interrogatory, say so, but make a reasonable and good faith effort to get the information by asking other persons or organizations, unless the information is equally available to the asking party.

(e) Whenever an interrogatory may be answered by referring to a document, the document may be attached as an exhibit to the response and referred to in the response. If the document has more than one page, refer to the page and section where the answer to the interrogatory can be found.

(f) Whenever an address and telephone number for the same person are requested in more than one interrogatory, you are required to furnish them in answering only the first interrogatory asking for that information.

(g) If you are asserting a privilege or making an objection to an interrogatory, you must specifically assert the privilege or state the objection in your written response.

(h) Your answers to these interrogatories must be verified, dated, and signed. You may wish to use the following form at the end of your answers:

I declare under penalty of perjury under the laws of the State of California that the foregoing answers are true and correct.

_____   _____
(DATE)   (SIGNATURE)

Sec. 4. Definitions
Words in **BOLDFACE CAPITALS** in these interrogatories are defined as follows:

(a) *(Check one of the following)*:
☐ (1) **INCIDENT** includes the circumstances and events surrounding the alleged accident, injury, or other occurrence or breach of contract giving rise to this action or proceeding.

Page 1 of 8

Form Approved for Optional Use
Judicial Council of California
DISC-001 [Rev. January 1, 2008]

FORM INTERROGATORIES—GENERAL

Code of Civil Procedure,
§§ 2030.010–2030.410, 2033.710
www.courtinfo.ca.gov

American LegalNet, Inc.
www.FormsWorkFlow.com

By contrast, special interrogatories are written questions you draft yourself. As such, special interrogatory questions are more specifically tailored to your case. The detriment is your questions may be more prone to objections. For example, if your question is unclear or compound, then the opposing party may object and refuse to answer.

To draft special interrogatories well, you need to know a few ground rules. First, you cannot ask compound questions, meaning no questions with "and" or "or." For example, a question like this wouldn't work: "Please state where you went after the car accident and where you were before the car accident."

The best-drafted questions are short, simple, and clear. For example: "State your relationship to Bob Smith."

Second, you cannot refer to information outside the question itself. For example, you cannot ask, "State all witnesses that support the complaint." Since the information contained in the complaint is not contained in your question (it is an outside document), your question need not be answered.

Third, you cannot ask about privileged information, such as attorney-client communications.

For these reasons, drafting up custom interrogatories is not so easy. But it can be done, and it does have a useful purpose.

Some lawyers use special interrogatories to ask about each contention listed in a complaint. For example, "If you contend that the parties had a written contract, state all witnesses who have knowledge of that written contract." This could be an effective way to find witnesses you do not know about. Unfortunately, many "contention interrogatories" are a waste of time because you will not receive any meaningful information from asking them. And you can bet that the other side will throw a slew of objections at you when they first answer your interrogatories. Why? Well, lawyers being lawyers, you will receive objections to interrogatories no matter what question you ask.

Even still, the better interrogatories you draft, the more likely you can overcome the objections and receive a proper answer. A little thought about the questions you want to ask goes a long way here. This is where an experienced guide—a lawyer—helps you obtain the evidence you need for trial. The lawyers at our firm, Albertson & Davidson, LLP, have drafted hundreds of thousands of interrogatories for our clients, and we can attest that experience counts when it comes to asking good questions.

Among the best uses for special interrogatories is when you have a specific question. For example, if you need to find out the name of a person's doctor, then you can ask a simple question, "State the name of your doctor." Once you have that name, you can issue a subpoena to the doctor to obtain medical records. This interrogatory is short and clear. If you receive an objection from the opposing party, you can easily deal with it. Ultimately, you are more likely to obtain the information you need from this simple question (assuming the person's doctor is relevant to the lawsuit), rather than asking a longer, more convoluted question.

As with all other written discovery, once interrogatories are served on the opposing party that party has thirty days in which to respond. Typically, extension of time is required and must be granted for a reasonable amount of time. If the responses to interrogatories are inadequate, then the "meet and confer" process must be used. If the opposition refuses to provide satisfactory answers, then a motion to compel is required to be filed with the court. See "discovery motions" in chapter 7.

Obtaining proper responses to interrogatories takes time, persistence, and a good deal of work. If you understand this point before heading into the written discovery phase of your lawsuit, then you will be better prepared to handle the slow road ahead.

Of course, the whole process would be much easier if your opponent would simply admit to the facts that benefit your case. Let's discuss how we may be able to accomplish that goal using requests for admissions.

CHAPTER 6

Written Discovery-
Requests for Admissions

Wouldn't it be nice if the opposing party just admitted they were wrong? That brings us to requests for admissions. Requests for admissions are unique in that they demand that the opposing party either admit or deny a given statement. As with interrogatories, these requests cannot be compound, nor refer to outside information.

Many parties will issue requests for admissions because they believe it is strategically advantageous to do so. You see, if a request for admission is denied, and that fact is later proven true at trial, then the denying party must pay the costs incurred to prove that fact true. This is an odd result of denying a request for admission, but it is meant to provide some consequence to giving a false denial.

For example, let's say you have a breach of contract lawsuit and everyone already agrees that a written contract was entered into between the parties. If you send a request for the other side to "admit the parties had a written contract," and that request is denied, it just wastes everyone's time having to prove that simple fact as being true during trial. That's why a party that denies a basic fact posed in a request for admissions must pay a penalty—to deter this wasting of time. We want parties to agree to some of the basic facts that are not in dispute to make trials more efficient.

The problem with most requests for admissions is that they are not well drafted. This means the other side can easily deny them without later being penalized or object to them and not answer at all.

The best use of requests for admissions is to admit the authenticity of documents. For example, if you send the opposing party a copy of your written contract and ask them to admit the document is genuine, and they do so, then you can easily admit that document into evidence at time of trial. And the opposing party probably wants to admit to the genuineness of the document because they want to use that same document in their case against you. In other words, it is an easy request to state, "Please admit the attached document is authentic." In fact, you can use the judicial council form for this purpose—they have a pre-printed form request for admission.

DISC-020

ATTORNEY OR PARTY WITHOUT ATTORNEY *(Name, State Bar number and address)*:	FOR COURT USE ONLY

TELEPHONE NO.:   FAX NO. *(Optional)*:
E-MAIL ADDRESS *(Optional)*:
ATTORNEY FOR *(Name)*:

SUPERIOR COURT OF CALIFORNIA, COUNTY OF
STREET ADDRESS:
MAILING ADDRESS:
CITY AND ZIP CODE:
BRANCH NAME:

SHORT TITLE:

REQUESTS FOR ADMISSION
☐ Truth of Facts   ☐ Genuineness of Documents
Requesting Party:
Answering Party:
Set No.:

CASE NUMBER:

INSTRUCTIONS

Requests for admission are written requests by a party to an action requiring that any other party to the action either admit or deny, under oath, the truth of certain facts or the genuineness of certain documents. For information on timing, the number of admissions a party may request from any other party, service of requests and responses, restrictions on the style, format, and scope of requests for admission and responses to requests, and other details, see Code of Civil Procedure sections 94–95, 1013, and 2033.010–2033.420 and the case law relating to those sections.

An answering party should consider carefully whether to admit or deny the truth of facts or the genuineness of documents. With limited exceptions, an answering party will not be allowed to change an answer to a request for admission. There may be penalties if an answering party fails to admit the truth of any fact or the genuineness of any document when requested to do so and the requesting party later proves that the fact is true or that the document is genuine. These penalties may include, among other things, payment of the requesting party's attorney's fees incurred in making that proof.

Unless there is an agreement or a court order providing otherwise, the answering party must respond in writing to requests for admission within 30 days after they are served, or within 5 days after service in an unlawful detainer action. There may be significant penalties if an answering party fails to provide a timely written response to each request for admission. These penalties may include, among other things, an order that the facts in issue are deemed true or that the documents in issue are deemed genuine for purposes of the case.

Answers to *Requests for Admission* must be given under oath. The answering party should use the following language at the end of the responses:

I declare under penalty of perjury under the laws of the State of California that the foregoing answers are true and correct.

(DATE)   *(SIGNATURE)*

These instructions are only a summary and are not intended to provide complete information about requests for admission. This *Requests for Admission* form does not change existing law relating to requests for admissions, nor does it affect an answering party's right to assert any privilege or to make any objection.

REQUESTS FOR ADMISSION

You are requested to admit within 30 days after service, or within 5 days after service in an unlawful detainer action, of this *Requests for Admission* that:

1. ☐ Each of the following facts is true *(if more than one, number each fact consecutively)*:

   ☐ Continued on Attachment 1

2. ☐ The original of each of the following documents, copies of which are attached, is genuine *(if more than one, number each document consecutively)*:

   ☐ Continued on Attachment 2

▶

(TYPE OR PRINT NAME)   *(SIGNATURE OF PARTY OR ATTORNEY)*

Page 1 of 1

You can also ask your opponent to admit any other fact of the case. For example, "Admit that the car accident occurred in Los Angeles." That's a simple fact that all parties could agree to without dispute. However, some facts will never be agreed to, such as "Admit that you breached the contract." If the lawsuit involves a breach of contract claim, then your opponent will never admit that request. So why make a request you know the other side will deny? Strategically it could set up your opponent to pay for a portion of your attorney's fees and costs if you prevail at time of trial. That rarely occurs, but some lawyers like to use that tactic in an attempt to build leverage against their opponent.

A bad example of a request for admission is when the request is convoluted. For example, "Admit that you did not receive any gift from your parent." This is a very broad request for admission. Does it mean never received any gift during your lifetime? What constitutes a "gift"? Do birthday cards count, or buying dinner? There is no timeframe for this request and no specific explanation of what a "gift" even means.

In these cases, the responding party has the option of doing a qualified admission. In other words, rather than just answering with "Admit," the responding party can say something like, "Objection to the request as being overbroad and vague; However, responding party does admit that he received birthday cards with twenty dollars enclosed every year from 1995 to 2015." The request did not ask that these specific facts be admitted, but the responding party can qualify their response and limit what they are willing to admit by doing so.

Drafting proper requests for admission is a bit of an art form. It takes time and clarity to draft them well. This is where an experienced guide can truly help. Our firm has drafted thousands of requests for admissions, so we have learned (sometimes the hard way) what works and what does not work when drafting requests for admissions. You must understand that drafting proper discovery requests, and obtaining proper answer to those requests, takes time and a lot of hard work. The sooner you accept this fact, the better you will handle the road ahead.

If a party admits a fact in response to a request for admission, that fact is considered proven true for all purposes at trial. If a request for admission is denied, then the facts contained in that particular request must be proven at trial. Again, if a received response is insufficient, the parties must first "meet and confer" and then file a motion to compel if the response is not adequate. That's what the next chapter covers, discovery motions, also called motions to compel.

CHAPTER 7

Written Discovery– Discovery Motions

D iscovery motions, also referred to as motions to compel, are the tool a party can use to seek court intervention with discovery. When a party fails to respond properly to a discovery request, the only way to force that party to comply with the discovery rules is by filing a discovery motion. The process can be simplified to: request, response, motion.

Unfortunately, filing a discovery motion with the court takes time, money, and luck. That means you must pay money, and your lawyer must work harder, just to obtain the information you are already entitled to under the Discovery Act. You must be prepared to encounter, and successfully overcome, these litigation roadblocks. Obtaining evidence is never easy.

The discovery motion must be filed within forty-five days of receiving a discovery response (which is extended five days if the response is served by mail, or two days if served by overnight delivery—see California Code of Procedure section 1005). But before filing a discovery motion, you must first meet and confer.

Before a motion can be filed, the parties must "meet and confer." The meet and confer process forces the parties (or the parties' attorneys if they are represented by attorneys) to discuss the problem before filing a motion in court. The hope is that the attorneys can work out a compromise that obviates the need for judicial intervention. Imagine that, lawyers agreeing to something … it could happen … maybe.

The meet and confer process can be done by letter, phone, or an in-person meeting between the lawyers. Letter is the most common method, and probably the best since it provides a written record of the issues addressed and the responses received.

The goal of meeting and conferring is to have a *meaningful* discussion of the issues. In other words, you need to have a reason for asking for better discovery responses from the opposing party. The discovery process is not supposed to be used to harass people (even though it often is used for this very purpose). And the meet and confer process is supposed to allow a robust discussion that has the potential to lead to compromise (even though it seems people rarely compromise). Compromise is found at times, which saves everyone the time and expense of filing a motion. The law requires you to at least try. So you must meet and confer.

If the parties cannot agree to a compromise after meeting and conferring on the discovery issue, then a motion to compel must be filed with the court. Generally speaking, the court disfavors motions to compel. Many judges view such motions as "two kids in a sandbox fighting over the toys." As such, parties must be certain that the items for which they are filing a motion are important and relevant to the lawsuit. Filing a motion for an irrelevant or unnecessary purpose is not only frowned upon by the court, but could also subject the moving party to sanctions for bringing the motion in the first instance.

Technically, the party who prevails on a motion to compel is awarded sanctions to compensate them for the attorneys' fees they spent to bring the motion. This rarely occurs. More often, the court either refuses to issue sanctions whatsoever or the amount of sanctions is nominal in comparison to the actual costs of the motion. Sometimes a party may not ask for sanctions for various strategic reasons. It all depends on your case and the issue for which you are seeking help from the court.

If you fail to file a motion to compel within forty-five days after you are served with discovery responses, then you are forever barred from seeking additional responses. That means the burden is on you to ensure the other side responds appropriately. And if they don't, you really can't complain about it after the deadline to file a motion to compel passes.

Informal Discovery Conferences

Judges do not like discovery motions any more than you do. They clog the court system with additional work and time to determine the proper ruling. And much of the time, a solution seems obvious to the judge, but not easily grasped by the parties, or their lawyers, due to the animosity that mounts between them throughout a lawsuit. As a result, the

California legislature enacted Code of Civil Procedure section 2016.080, which authorizes the court to conduct informal discovery conferences.

An informal discovery conference is a meeting between the judge assigned to your case and the lawyers where the discovery matters in dispute can be discussed and possibly resolved voluntarily. By "voluntarily" we mean that the judge will not make a forced ruling at the meeting. Rather, the judge will give their view of the issue and then ask the parties to come to an agreement. Obviously, if your judge is giving their view of your discovery dispute, you should listen to what they are saying. This is the same person who will rule on your discovery motion if you do not come to a voluntary agreement with your opponent, so the judge's view of the issue should carry great weight in your mind.

Either party, or the court on its own prerogative, can request an informal discovery conference. The party making the request files a declaration with the court, and the opposing party can respond with their own declaration. The court is supposed to schedule the informal discovery conference within thirty days of a party making the request. The court also has the power to extend the deadline by which to file a discovery motion—this is great because it prevents the parties from spending time and money preparing a discovery motion before the conference takes place. In our experience, once people spend time and money on a discovery motion, they are far less likely to agree to a compromise.

The informal discovery conference procedure was enacted as of January 1, 2018. While our firm has used the process a few times, it remains to be seen whether this process will help discovery disputes in the long run. So far, our experience has indicated that these conferences will be a great success. The informal meetings save time, money, and reduce

animosity between the lawyers. With so many formal processes that slow down and complicate a lawsuit, having a de-
vice like informal discovery conferences may help simplify
and streamline your lawsuit—a positive change.

The Motion Process

If you still require the filing of a discovery motion, the process starts with you (or your lawyer) drafting the motion that
sets out your issue. You are also required to prepare and file
a separate statement that lists each of the discovery demands you made, the response that was given, and the reason why that response is inadequate. The separate
statement can be a big undertaking if you asked a lot of questions. For example, if you have one hundred document demands and you want to compel on each of them, then you
must separately state each of the one hundred demands you
made, the response to each of those one hundred demands,
and the reason why each of those responses requires a further response.

Once you have your motion on file, don't be surprised if
the opposing party files a response and asks for sanctions
against you for filing the motion in the first place. The court
has the power to issue sanctions against the losing party in a
discovery motion. That means you, as the moving party (the
person who filed the motion to compel), could end up paying
the opposing party if you lose your discovery motion. This is
another reason why you want to have a sound legal basis for
filing your motion to compel. If you are filing a motion that is
not supported by legal authority, then you are more likely to
be sanctioned by the court.

The discovery process is supposed to allow each party an
equal and fair chance to gather relevant evidence prior to

conducting a trial. And in many cases, the discovery process meets this goal. But discovery is not successfully accomplished without a few fights along the way. And you rarely will obtain all the evidence you hope to have. But you can obtain far more evidence under the discovery rules than would otherwise be available if we had no discovery rules at all. You must be prepared to fight for the evidence you need, but also compromise where the evidence is not likely to be obtained.

We have discussed the basics you should know about the discovery process. Now let's cover more specifically what your obligations are when it comes to written discovery.

CHAPTER 8

Written Discovery– Your Obligations

Now that we have discussed written discovery, in general, let's discuss your obligations when it comes to written discovery. There are some requirements that you are personally subjected to when you become a party to a lawsuit. And it is important that you know what some of these requirements are, so you can comply with them.

You are not obligated to serve written discovery on anyone—sending discovery requests to anyone is voluntary on your part. Throughout your lawsuit, however, there will be times when the opposing party will serve you with written discovery. And your response to written discovery requests is mandatory. Your attorneys will receive that discovery on your behalf, if you have hired attorneys, but they will need your help to respond to discovery.

If you choose not to respond, the court has the power to impose onerous sanctions on you, which can include forcing you to pay a monetary fine, finding certain issues against you, or allowing your opponent to win the case without a trial. The punishments are far worse than the burden on responding. So be sure to participate in your discovery responses.

We will go through each of the written discovery devices we discussed thus far in section 2 and point out some of the obligations you have when responding.

Document Demands

Document demands, also known as "requests for production of documents and tangible things," obligate you to allow the opposing party to review and inspect documents in your possession, custody, or control that are relevant to the lawsuit, and not subject to a reasonable objection. What the heck does all that mean? Let's break it down into two categories: (1) what you must do, and (2) what you needn't do.

1.   What You Must Do

You must determine what documents you have in your possession that meet the type of documents requested by the opposing party. If the document demand references "all medical records for Mr. John Smith from January 1, 2017 to January 1, 2018," then you should start by determining if you have any medical documents that meet that description. If you do, then you may be obligated to provide those documents, or copies of those documents, to the opposing party.

Even if the documents are not in your possession, you still may have an obligation to provide documents that are within your "custody or control." Custody or control refers to documents that you can access because you have them located somewhere that you control, or with someone you control.

For example, if you gave financial documents to your accountant, that accountant is essentially your agent. That agent in under your control, and you can obtain the financial documents from your agent simply by asking for them back. As such, you still have an obligation to obtain copies of those documents for the opposing party if those documents are requested. The fact that you do not have physical possession of the documents at the time the document demand is served on you is irrelevant because you still control those documents even though they are with your accountant.

The same would be true of documents that are stored in a bank safe-deposit box or in an off-site storage unit. You may not have them in your home, but you control your safe-deposit box and your off-site storage unit, so you have an obligation to obtain the documents.

You must provide all relevant documents to the opposing party. Technically, the opposing party has the right to inspect and copy the documents if they choose to do so. But practically speaking this is not how it works. In most cases, you will simply make a copy of the documents and provide those copies to the opposing party. It is much easier on you to do this, rather than being forced to appear at some office with your documents and wait around while the documents are reviewed and copied.

2.   What You Needn't Do

You only have to provide documents that are requested by the opposing attorney. You may have documents that you think are relevant to the lawsuit. If so, be sure to give those to your attorneys. But if the opposing party does not ask for the documents, then you have no obligation to provide them copies.

You have no obligation to procure documents that are not currently in your possession, custody, or control. For example, if you are asked for medical records that are with your doctor's office, but you don't have copies of them, then you have no obligation to obtain those documents. You can merely state in your response to the document demand that you have no such documents in your possession, custody, or control. Also, your medical records are protected by your Constitutional Right to Privacy, so the medical records won't be obtained by your opponent unless they are directly relevant to your lawsuit. If the opposing party still wants those documents, then they can subpoena the doctor's office for them. If your opponent subpoenas the doctor's office for your medical records, and you don't think they should receive a copy of them, then you can bring a motion with the court seeking an order to protect those records from disclosure. Notice that all of this is done under the Discovery Act and the subpoena process.

You also have no obligation to produce documents for which your attorney has a legitimate objection. The most common example would be attorney-client privileged documents. Let's say you sent your lawyer a letter discussing your case or your lawyer sent you a letter. That communication is protected by the attorney-client privilege. If you receive a document demand asking for all letters discussing the case, you may have to produce any letters you sent to your friend,

YOUR LAWSUIT • 65

but you don't have to produce any letters you sent to your lawyer. Your lawyer will object to the document demand on the basis of the attorney-client privilege, and you will have no obligation to produce the letter to the opposing party.

Finally, you have no obligation to produce irrelevant documents. It is not uncommon for document demands to be drafted in a way that is overly broad. When that occurs, you have the right to object to the demand as being overly broad. In those cases, the attorney will usually discuss a plan to allow some documents to be produced, but not everything under the sun. You should talk with your lawyer if you feel a request is too broad.

The Response

When a document demand is received, you are required to respond to that demand within thirty days. The response (1) informs the other side of which demands you will respond to by providing documents, (2) sets forth any objections, and (3) states whether any demands will not be complied with. Any demands that fall under (3) must also have a statement explaining why you will not comply with the request. You must state that (a) you do not possess the documents, (b) the documents have never existed, or (c) the documents have been lost or destroyed. Your lawyer should prepare this response for you to review.

You then will need to sign a verification, which is a statement under penalty of perjury that the contents of the response are true (as discussed in chapter 1). Since you are signing under penalty of perjury, you should read the response to be sure you agree with it. If you see anything in the response that you believe to be inaccurate, then you should contact your attorney immediately.

Producing the Documents

Producing the documents often occurs at the same time as sending the response. And usually you will copy the relevant documents or save them onto a computer disk or flash drive, and send them to the opposing party with the response. However, there are times when you may want to request that the opposing party either retrieve the documents or come to your attorney's office to review them. You don't need to worry about how the documents are produced because your lawyer will do that for you. Your only obligation in this process is to provide your lawyer with all relevant documents.

Important reminder: any relevant documents NOT produced when requested in a document demand may be barred from use at trial. For this reason, producing all relevant documents, especially those you want to use at trial, is critically important.

Interrogatories

When you receive interrogatories from an opposing party, you have a lot of questions you need to answer. As with document demands, your attorneys may have some objections to the questions being asked. If so, there may be some questions you only have to answer partially, and others you won't answer at all.

Absent a relevant objection, however, you're obligated to make a good faith attempt to answer the question presented. Remember that interrogatories come in two formats: special interrogatories and form interrogatories. In other words, questions drafted by the opposing attorney (special interrogatories) and questions provided on a pre-printed form prepared by the California Judicial Council (form inter-rogatories).

Basically, all interrogatories are the same in that they ask a written question and you are expected to provide a written answer. The answer is prepared with the help of your attor-ney, so you are not required to answer the interrogatories by yourself. Some interrogatories are simple, such as, "State your address." Others are more complicated, such as, "State all facts that support your contention that the defendant breached your alleged written contract." For this reason, at-torneys are allowed to help draft a written response to each interrogatory.

As the client, you should review the written interrogatories and provide your version of the answer as best you can. The lawyer can then take that information and prepare the final written response. Don't be surprised if your lawyer leaves out some of the information you provide or they provide ad-ditional information—that's normal. But be sure that all facts stated in the answers to interrogatories are accurate, to the best of your knowledge, because you will be required to ver-ify that the answers are true and correct. That verification is given under penalty of perjury (see chapter 1), so if an an-swer is knowingly false, you could be in trouble.

As with all other written discovery, once interrogatories are served on you, you have thirty days in which to respond to them in writing. That time period may be extended by agreement of the attorneys—and it often is extended de-pending on the number of interrogatories asked of you.

Answering interrogatories can be tedious and time-con-suming. But well-drafted responses are important to ensure your obligations under the California Discovery Act. Be prepared for both your lawyer and yourself to spend time, and money, crafting proper responses to discovery. If you understand this point, then the process will be much easier for you to handle.

Requests for Admissions

Requests for admissions are unique in that they demand that you either admit or deny the statement made in each request. Requests for admissions (referred to as RFAs) are not always used, but when they are received, a proper response must be drafted. As with interrogatories, there may be objections to some of the requests, which will obviate the need for a response. Also, you are allowed to have your attorney assist you with responding to RFAs.

You actually have three options when responding to RFAs. You can admit the request as being true, you can deny the request, or you can state that you do not have enough information to admit or deny. Of course, this third option must be true. You must verify your responses to RFAs under penalty of perjury, so be sure not to lie or provide false answers.

Be advised that there is a consequence to denying an RFA that is later proven true at time of trial—you have to pay the costs of the opposing party. For example, if you are asked to admit that you entered into a written contract with the plaintiff, and you did, in fact, enter into a written contract, but you deny that request just to be difficult, you could end up paying for that denial. If the plaintiff later proves that you did enter into a written contract during trial, then you could be forced to pay the plaintiff's attorneys' fees for their having to spend time and money proving the written contract was true. For these reasons, you must be careful when denying an RFA. Be sure your denial is truthful. If you can admit an RFA because it is asking you to admit something you do not dispute, then it is much safer to simply admit that RFA as true.

As previously mentioned, RFAs are often used to admit the authenticity of documents. Using the written contract example, the plaintiff may ask you to admit a written contract is the authentic document that you signed. If the document is authentic and correct, then you would likely admit that RFA as being true—yes, that is the correct contract both parties signed. If both parties admit to the authenticity of a document, then it can easily be admitted as evidence during trial. If you also want to use the contract for your case when you go to trial, then admitting its authenticity also makes it easier for you to admit the contract as evidence.

Obviously, there is a lot of legal strategy in responding to RFAs. There are consequences for improper denials, there are document authentication issues, there are times when you can't admit or deny a request. You need to spend time with your lawyer working through these issues to be sure you are ready to properly respond to RFAs when the time comes.

Supplemental Responses

After you have spent time going through all of the discovery requests sent to you and paid your lawyer to prepare your responses to discovery, the opposing party is probably going to ask you to do it all again. This brings us to the topic of supplemental responses.

Your initial response to discovery is usually going to be prepared by your lawyer to protect you as much as possible. That means the lawyer is going to include all manner of objections to many of the requests, and perhaps even refuse to respond to any number of requests that are made to you.

Your lawyer is not trying to break the rules or be difficult. Let's refer to the first set of responses as "conservative." In other words, why give all sorts of information and evidence to the opposing party if you can get away with giving less? There's only one way to test out how much you can get away with, and that's by giving "conservative" responses. Your opponent will probably give you conservative responses at first too. The opposing party will call your responses "insufficient," "bereft of facts," and "an abuse of the discovery process." Let the games begin! The more you anticipate the bumps in store for you and your case, the better you will be at handling the rough spots.

This is how discovery works in our legal system. The plaintiff asks for information. The defendant provides some information, but not everything that may be required. The plaintiff demands supplemental responses. The same is true if you begin with the defendant asking for information. The name of the game seems to be: say little, and then say a little bit more. This is not always the case. There certainly are times when a party will properly, and fully, answer discovery. But there are more times when a party will be asked to supplement their initial discovery responses.

Supplemental responses are simply a second set of responses where a few of the objections are removed, more information is given, a few more documents are exchanged, and maybe a response or two to an RFA is changed from "deny" to "admit."

It is typical that discovery responses will be supplemented at least once, and sometimes two or three times before they become final. If the parties disagree on a proper response, and they refuse to supplement the responses, then a discovery motion is required to seek court intervention to settle the dispute.

Discovery Motions

Discovery motions, also referred to as motions to compel, are a rather common occurrence in most lawsuits. They certainly are filed more often than the court would like, but we digress. Let's discuss your role in discovery motions.

Discovery motions come after discovery has been responded to, a party is not satisfied with the response for some reason, the parties have "met and conferred" to work out their dispute, and there is no compromise between the parties (or attorneys). In other words, discovery motions are the last step in the process to procure information from the opposing party.

There are times when your lawyer will file a discovery motion against the other side, and times when other parties will file a discovery motion against you. At this point, the issues are usually legally based as to why the response is not sufficient. There is rarely a time when you, as the client, have to provide much input on the discovery motion. It is a lawyer thing, and the lawyers need to fight it out.

Whenever any party receives verified responses to discovery, they only have forty-five days in which to file a discovery motion if they believe further responses are required. As already given, the forty-five-day deadline is extended by five days if the discovery motion is served by mail, and two days if served by overnight delivery.

Your only obligation at the discovery motion stage is to foot the bill. Unfortunately, discovery motions take time to prepare and/or respond to, and time means money. In theory, the prevailing party to a discovery motion is supposed to be paid for their attorneys' fees by the losing party, but that rarely occurs. Often the court will not order any attorneys' fees to be paid to you (or by you, if you lose the discovery motion), or the court will award an amount that is much less than what you actually paid your lawyer to prepare and respond to the discovery motion.

Discovery motions are necessary evils in most lawsuits because there is no other way to force an opposing party to properly respond to discovery. As a result, the discovery motion must be used when responses are insufficient.

Section 2- Brief

We are now leaving the world of written discovery where you are asking written questions, seeking documents, and asking for written responses. That's all the subject of the prior chapters. You should know by now that you never know as much information as you'd like when preparing a lawsuit. Obtaining evidence is chaotic, expensive, time-consuming, and incomplete. But still, you must try your best. If you prepare yourself for the chaos, particularly with the help of a great law firm—think Albertson & Davidson, LLP—the process is much easier to handle. Work hard, persist in your efforts, obtain as much evidence as possible (or financially feasible), and then proceed to the next phase of your lawsuit.

We now turn to depositions, the world of live testimony.

Section 3

The Discovery Phase: Depositions

The discovery phase continues with a focus on depositions. A deposition is the live questioning of a witness under oath with a court reporter present. You will learn how depositions work and your obligations for your deposition.

CHAPTER 9

Depositions

A deposition is the live questioning of a witness under oath with a court reporter present. Depositions are typically scheduled once the written discovery is complete or near completion although this is just custom not dictated by the discovery rules. In fact, you can take a deposition any time you like after your lawsuit has been filed.

For most depositions, your lawyer will sit down across from the witness and ask them questions. It is the same as a direct or cross-examination that occurs in court at time of trial. The only difference being there is no judge present. The witness has the right to have their lawyer present to state any legal objection to the questions being asked. Expect to find more on legal objections a little later.

Each party to the lawsuit also has the right to be present during all depositions, along with the party's lawyer. And finally, you will have a court reporter present to transcribe the questions and answers, so they can be used throughout the lawsuit and at time of trial for limited purposes. Some depositions are also videotaped. In that event, the video operator will also be present in the room during the deposition.

In California, each witness can only be questioned for seven hours. You can ask for more time by filing a motion with the court, or the parties can agree to more time voluntarily. But the seven-hour limitation is set by statute and forms the basic timeframe for which a deposition can last.

Also, each witness is only required to sit for their deposition once. Even if that deposition lasts multiple days, it is still considered part of a single deposition session. Once the deposition ends, the witness cannot be questioned again at a deposition, unless the court orders a second deposition (which is rare). The only other time the witness will be compelled to answer questions under oath during live questioning is at trial.

Given these constraints, it is important that you or your lawyer spends sufficient time to properly prepare to take the deposition before it occurs. You have limited time to ask questions, and you usually are going to have only one shot at taking the deposition. This is why depositions typically occur after the written discovery is final because there could be documents and other information you find during written discovery that you can then use during questioning at deposition.

If you were to take a deposition, and then find a document afterwards that you want to ask about, you would be out of luck. Once the deposition ends, there can be no more questioning until time of trial.

Further, the questions you want to ask must be prepared as well. That's not to say that every question must be written down in advance, but certainly subject areas you want to ask about should be outlined and prepared. In many instances a lawyer will spend far more time preparing for a deposition than the time itself spent at the deposition asking questions. Our firm, Albertson & Davidson, LLP, has conducted thousands of depositions over the years, so we know how to ask proper deposition questions. But more than that, we have refined our strategy when conducting a deposition. Feel free to contact the authors if you have any questions, or need any assistance, with your depositions. We have talked about how experience counts in this book, and we can't emphasize that enough. It is called the "practice of law" for a reason: because you never really stop practicing, and hopefully improving, your skills.

Depositions can be taken of parties and third-party witnesses. The only limitation is that the witness must be at least eighteen years of age, mentally competent to provide testimony, and have personal knowledge of the facts being asked about at the deposition—or be an expert witness if being asked to give an expert opinion.

If you are a party to a lawsuit, you have the right, but not the obligation, to attend any deposition occurring in your case.

Unfortunately, most depositions do not play out like a television show. You rarely have a "gotcha" moment or a damaging admission by the witness. That isn't really the purpose of a deposition anyway. It would be nice if those things did occur at deposition, but they usually don't.

The real reason for depositions is to preserve testimony and give you an idea of how someone will testify come time of trial. Discovery is meant to eliminate, or at least minimize, surprises at trial. If you know how someone will testify at trial before they take the witness stand, it is a big advantage, hence, the purpose of taking depositions.

By the way, don't be surprised if a witness tells you one thing before a deposition and then testifies differently while under oath at deposition. That sort of thing happens all the time. For some reason people have a tendency to change their story, and dramatically reduce their assertions, when under oath. Many people are surprised when a friendly witness tells them something favorable for their case, only to hear that same person say something less glowing at deposition. It all comes with the territory.

During the deposition one lawyer at a time is allowed to ask questions of the witness. The witness' attorney is allowed to make objections to the form of the question. In other words, the attorney is not supposed to object to the content of the question although that does happen. A proper objection might be that the question is vague or compound. For example, if a witness were asked, "When did you eat lunch?" that question is vague if not given some context of what day or time period you are referencing. "When did you eat lunch yesterday?" would be a more appropriate (and less vague) question.

Questions also cannot be compound. "Were you married and were you divorced?" is a compound question. The answer could be yes to one and no to the other. The question would be more appropriate by simply stating each part separately: "Were you married?" followed by "Were you divorced?"

While the witness' lawyer will state objections for the record, there is no judge there to decide whether the objection is valid or not. As a result, the witness is still expected to answer the question even after an objection is made. If ever the deposition transcript is used in court, then the judge can rule on the objection. You must state the objection during questions to preserve the objection for a judge to maybe rule on at a later time. It is a bit strange, but that's how it works. In fact, you will see as we continue that most aspects of a deposition are confusing and certainly chaotic. Be prepared to encounter these difficulties as part of your lawsuit.

Once the deposition is complete, the court reporter will prepare a written transcript. You will have an opportunity to review your own deposition testimony and the deposition testimony of all other witnesses. The transcript can be used to prepare for court filing, trial, and other depositions. Sometimes a deposition will bring to light other documentary evidence that can be subpoenaed. Deposition testimony can be useful in countless ways.

Generally, deposition testimony cannot be used at trial. In our court system, the witness must testify in person at trial, and all parties must have the right to cross-examine that witness in court. However, if a witness testifies differently at trial than they did at their deposition, then that person's deposition testimony can be read into the record at trial in order to prove that their testimony is inconsistent.

There are other limited exceptions to when deposition testimony can be used at trial. For example, if a witness is unavailable come time of trial, then excerpts of the deposition testimony can be read into the record at trial as well.

Finally, there are times when disputes arise as to what a witness can or cannot testify to at deposition. Witnesses may refuse to answer questions or be directed by their attorneys not to answer questions. When that occurs, again, the parties must meet and confer in an attempt to resolve their differences. If an agreement is not reached, then a discovery motion (motion to compel) is required (see chapter 7). The party demanding the answers would usually file a discovery motion and seek a court order that the witness appear at deposition again and answer the specific questions that were not answered at the initial deposition.

Alternatively, if the witness' lawyer feels the witness is being harassed in a way that is not appropriate under the discovery rules, then they can suspend the deposition and file their own discovery motion (called a motion for protective order) seeking a court order that the witness need not answer certain questions or need not have any further deposition testimony.

It all depends on the facts and circumstances of your matter. The point is that when depositions don't go well, the parties are back to the discovery motion option.

If you hire a lawyer, then you will not have any obligation in preparing to take the deposition of a witness. Your lawyer will do that for you. It never hurts to discuss the witness with your lawyer. Also, you can expect that at some point in your lawsuit, you will be deposed. That's what the next chapter discusses.

CHAPTER 10

Depositions- Your Obligations

At some point in your lawsuit, you will be deposed. In that event—and you should expect it to happen—you need to know some of the ground rules for giving testimony at deposition. Some of the following issues are things you must do, and others are suggestions to help you give your best deposition testimony.

Preparing for Your Deposition

It all starts with the truth. Your deposition testimony will be taken under oath, which means you promise to tell the truth under penalty of perjury. You don't need to be worried, the truth is easy for you to tell. Just stick to the facts you know and you'll be fine.

If you are a party to a lawsuit, you will receive a notice of taking deposition (or rather your lawyer will receive it). Your lawyer should notify you of the date, time, and place for the deposition. You will also want to schedule some time to meet with your lawyer before the deposition takes place.

It pays to take some time with your lawyer to prepare for your deposition. While every case is different, and every deposition is different, here are six pointers to keep in mind, so you can give your best deposition.

Pointer 1: Remember, You are Not Alone

Your attorneys will defend you at your deposition. By defending, your attorneys will voice relevant objections to the questions being asked of you when they deem it prudent to do so. Your attorneys will also ensure that the opposing counsel does not harass you or ask you questions that are protected by any privileges—such as the attorney-client privilege.

You should feel confident in knowing that you are not alone at your deposition. And you are allowed to take breaks throughout the deposition period. If you need a break, just ask. Your attorney will be sure you have the breaks you need to give your best evidence.

If you have a medical condition of any sort that makes it difficult for you to give deposition testimony for long periods of time, then breaks are even more important. Talk to your lawyer about your medical needs, so they can be discussed with the opposing attorneys and a compromise can be reached to accommodate your medical needs. Alternatively, if the opposing attorneys refuse to accommodate your medical needs, then your lawyer can file a motion for protective order and ask the court to order the attorneys to provide you with your required accommodations.

Pointer 2: Do Not Volunteer Information

This is the seminal rule of having your deposition taken: only answer the questions that are asked. Never volunteer additional information. This is also one of the hardest rules to follow because it's the opposite of what we typically do in social conversations.

For example, if you are at a social gathering and someone asks you, "Do you live around here?" you might answer, "No, actually I live about thirty miles away, but I have only lived there for five years because I was born and raised in Colorado." This is a fine response in a social setting because we understand that it would be rude to force someone to ask us twenty questions to obtain information. We want and expect people to fill in the gaps for us, and we do the same for them.

But at deposition, if you are asked, "Do you live around here?" the proper answer is "No," and that's it. The other information can be given if it is asked for, and ONLY if it is asked for. Thus, the person conducting the deposition may then ask, "Where do you live?" to which you would answer, "About thirty miles away." If the questioning continues with, "How long have you lived there?" then you can respond, "For five years." At a deposition you give the information only as it is asked even though it may not feel normal—because it's not normal. Few things about depositions relate to your normal life outside of this lawsuit. The better you are prepared for this chaotic experience, the better you will perform.

Almost every witness ever deposed in the history of law-yer-kind has violated this rule. You will too. But try to stick with the rule as best you can. You may even want to practice with a friend or family member beforehand to train yourself not to say anything more than is asked. If you find yourself talking more than you should at your deposition, then just stop. Your lawyer may even remind you to only answer the question that is asked. You will get the hang of it eventually.

Pointer 3: If You Don't Know, Say So

You are required to answer all relevant questions at your deposition, unless your lawyer directs you not to answer a question based on your right to privacy or privilege (such as the attorney-client privilege). Your obligation is to state what you know as you are sitting at your deposition. You are not required to remember every fact asked of you. That would be impossible. Therefore, there will be times during your deposition when you are asked a question to which you do not know the answer. If that occurs, simply say you don't know. Saying, "I don't know," is a proper answer as long as it is truthful. If you know the answer but say you don't, that would be a lie and improper in a deposition setting.

But the law also doesn't expect you to know every little de-tail and fact asked of you either. For example, if someone asks me, "What did you have for breakfast on this day five years ago?" my response is "I don't know." That is a truthful answer because I honestly have no idea what I had for break-fast five years ago.

After saying, "I don't know," the opposing attorney may show you a document or other information in an attempt to jog your memory. If this occurs, you should review the docu-ment or information carefully, and then answer the question as best you can.

Pointer 4: You May Estimate, but Never Guess

There are times when you may not know an answer with certainty, but the opposing attorney will ask you to estimate. Making reasonable estimations is acceptable at a deposition, but guessing is not. You should never guess at an answer at a deposition. Either you know the answer, or you don't (in which case you say, "I don't know").

But you can provide a reasonable estimate. For example, take the question, "On what exact date did you buy your last car?" You may respond, "I don't know." The follow-up question might be, "Was it within the last five years?" to which you could respond, "Yes." Estimating the purchase of your last car to be within the last five years is a reasonable estimation and an acceptable answer.

In contrast, if you were asked, "When was the exact date one of the authors of this book bought his last car?" you would have no way of knowing or even estimating an answer to that question (unless you were with one of us when we were buying a car). That is the difference between a reasonable estimation and a guess. An estimation has some connection to your personal knowledge of past events. Remember, you should never guess. If you think you would be making a guess, simply say so.

Pointer 5: Pause Before Each Answer

You're not the only one performing at your deposition. Your lawyer also has a role to play and a few objections to make along the way. When the deposing attorney poses a question, your lawyer may choose to voice an objection to the form of that question. Your lawyer's objection is supposed to be stated before you answer. And there may even be times when your lawyer instructs you not to answer a question, such as when the objection is based on attorney-client privilege.

As a result, you should pause for several seconds before answering each question. This slight pause will allow your lawyer time to state an objection if they have one. Again, pausing before answering is hard to do because it is not natural, but it is necessary and helpful. If you find pausing difficult, then try counting to two before answering the stated question.

Pointer 6: Know Your Lawsuit

Before your deposition, be sure you understand the legal claims you are making in court and why you are making those claims. We don't mean you should know the legalese of the lawsuit. You are not a lawyer and will not be expected to know legal issues (even if you are a lawyer sitting for a deposition, you usually are not expected to testify on legal issues). But you are a witness who knows the facts of your case, or you should know the facts of your case.

For example, assume you entered into a written contract with Bob where you were going to sell Bob your car and Bob was going to pay you $250 per month. Bob pays for two months and then stops paying. You sue Bob for breach of contract and ask for the rest of the payment due to you. If you are sitting for your deposition in the case against Bob, and Bob's attorney asks you, "Why did you bring this lawsuit?" you had better know. You might answer, "To obtain the rest of the payments Bob owes me, of course!"

Unfortunately, there are times when people don't seem to know why they filed a lawsuit. That's not a good sign. At a minimum, you need to know the story of your case. You should know that story since you lived it. Even if you don't understand the law, you should understand the facts that make up your story. If you were disinherited from your parent's estate, you should know the facts of your relationship with your parent.

In other words, be sure you understand why you brought your lawsuit and what are you looking to accomplish by filing your lawsuit. This is a discussion you should have with your lawyer prior to your deposition.

Don't worry about your deposition. If you sit down, tell the truth, and answer the question that is asked, you'll do fine. Some preparation with your lawyer will help you tremendously, so be sure to schedule time to do that before your deposition takes place.

Section 3 Brief

Depositions are one of the most effective methods to obtain evidence and establish a witness' testimony prior to trial. But as with all other issues relating to your lawsuit, depositions are strange at first blush. The procedures are confusing, and the process is time-consuming. Now that you know something about depositions, however, you should be better prepared for the difficulties you will encounter during the deposition phase of litigation.

Now that you have gathered some evidence, you will be expected to attend some form of settlement talks. That brings us to the mediation/settlement phase.

Section 4

The Mediation/Settlement Phase

Two of the most common settlement conference methods used in civil and probate matters are mandatory settlement conferences and mediation. Section 4 dedicates a chapter to each and explains how each works, its benefits, and its downsides.

CHAPTER 11

Mandatory Settlement Conferences

At some point throughout your lawsuit the court will either ask or order you to attend some form of settlement conference. Sometimes, the parties will agree voluntarily to attend in hopes of reaching a settlement. It is estimated that around 97% of all civil cases (including civil, trust, will, and probate matters) settle before trial. There are many factors that lead parties to settle, but one of the biggest factors is the use of mandatory settlement conferences and mediation in lawsuits. This chapter discusses the first and the following chapter discusses the latter.

MSC

Mandatory settlement conferences, as the name denotes, are mandatory. A mandatory settlement conference is often referred to by lawyers and court personnel as an "MSC" for short. Every court handles MSCs differently. In fact, courts are constantly trying to improve the MSC process, so even the same court may handle MSCs differently at different times, or in the context of different lawsuits.

One aspect that is the same for all MSCs is that they are meant to help facilitate a voluntary settlement between the parties to a lawsuit. By voluntary, we mean that the resolution is not forced on any one party. You'll see later that the same is true of mediations.

MSCs are conducted at the courthouse with court personnel. Sometimes you will meet with a judge, a lawyer who volunteers their time to negotiate settlement conferences, or some other person who will act as a neutral negotiator for the parties.

Typically, the parties will meet with a judge. Not the judge that is assigned to your case, but a different judge at the courthouse. In many cases, the judge will ask the lawyers to step into the judge's chambers (office) to discuss the case. The judge will then talk to each party's lawyer separately to determine what offer that party is willing to make to settle the matter. The judge then relays that information to the other party. The judge will go back and forth between the lawyers exchanging each party's offer to settle.

The process is similar when conducted by a non-judge. The point is, someone will meet with the parties, or the parties' attorneys, and discuss settlement offers.

Going back to our hypothetical breach of contract case against Bob, if you were at an MSC, Bob's lawyer may tell ¹ judge (or neutral negotiator, whoever that is) that Bob wi settle the case by making a payment to you of $250. If th

for the court to conduct the MSC. That is a great benefit to you.

Since MSCs are conducted at the courthouse, they usually only last until 4:30 or 5:00 in the afternoon because the court closes around that time. This means that MSCs tend to take less time than other settlement methods, such as mediation.

It is fairly common that a court will order the parties to attend an MSC, so whatever your view of them, you probably will be required to attend the MSC.

MSC Downsides

The first downside is that MSCs require your physical presence in court. You must be at the MSC by order of the court, in most cases. If you live a long way away from the courthouse where your lawsuit is pending, you will be expected to travel to court for the MSC. That's just the way things go in lawsuits.

Moreover, MSCs tend to be less effective than a private mediation because the court often has to conduct several MSCs at the same time. In other words, the judge may be talking to multiple parties from several lawsuits. You may just be one of many lawsuits that have an MSC scheduled at that time. So you may not receive the undivided attention of the judge or neutral negotiator the way you would at a private mediation.

Since MSCs end when the courthouse closes, they tend to be shorter. This can be bad if negotiations are progressing, but a deal is not yet reached come closing time. With a private mediation, your mediator will usually stay as long as is required to settle the case. Judges don't have that luxury because the courtroom personnel have to leave at the end of the day when the courthouse closes—no exceptions.

At Albertson & Davidson, LLP, we have successfully settled many cases using the MSC process, but we have also failed to settle many cases at MSC as well. You see, it can be a mixed bag in terms of the type of MSC process encountered and the ability of that process to help the parties broker a successful settlement. In our experience, private mediations tend to work better—not always, but more often than not. If you have any further questions about an upcoming conference and mediation, please contact the authors or visit us online: www.aldavlaw.com.

With that, let's now discuss mediations and you can then decide for yourself which process sounds more appealing to you.

CHAPTER 12

Mediation

Mediation is an informal meeting between the parties and a neutral third party called a "mediator." The mediator is usually a retired judge or a practicing lawyer with some expertise in the area of law at issue in your case. Mediations usually last a full day. The meeting usually takes place at either the mediator's office or a lawyer's office. Sometimes parties will attend mediation voluntarily, with each party agreeing to participate in hopes of settling the case. However, mediation can also be ordered by the court.

Here's the setup of mediations: parties are placed in separate rooms, and the mediator moves back and forth between the parties attempting to reach a compromise between the parties. If the parties do not voluntarily come to an agreement, then the mediation ends and the lawsuit continues in court. In other words, mediation does not result in a forced or involuntary result or ruling. The mediator is simply trying to come to a brokered agreement—not make any final or binding decisions in your case.

Even if mediation is not "ordered" by the court, the court often leans heavily on parties to attend at least one mediation before their trial date is set. In fact, some courts will only give priority for trial setting to parties who have attended mediation. Courts prefer that parties come to a voluntary settlement rather than using precious judicial resources to conduct a trial.

What Mediation is NOT

Mediation is NOT a forum for deciding your dispute. In other words, the mediator will not make a decision or make any suggestions to the court as to who should prevail. The mediator is merely a neutral negotiator. The mediator's job is to help each party see the strengths of the opposing party's case and the weaknesses of their own case, and propose possible ways in which the matter could be settled before trial.

Mediation is also not a forum for justice. The mediator will not decide who is right and who is wrong. Instead, the mediator focuses on a financial solution, with the intent of reaching a voluntary settlement between the parties. If a voluntary settlement is not reached between the parties, then the mediation ends and the lawsuit continues as before.

Good Old Fashioned Horse Trading

We often tell clients that mediation is nothing more than horse-trading. You offer to give someone something in return for dropping the lawsuit. It's just that simple. Stated another way, mediation is like a pie: everyone needs a slice to settle the case. The only question: how big of a slice must you give away to get the rest of the pie for yourself?

Many people (clients and lawyers alike) make the mistaken assumption that mediation is a great time to argue about the legal theories of the case. Based on our 3.5 decades of combined experience, we disagree. Our firm, Albertson & Davidson, LLP, has handled hundreds, maybe thousands, of mediations, and we have learned that the best way to obtain a great settlement is to focus on the task at hand—settling. By the time you reach mediation, the lawyers likely already have argued over the legal theories of the case quite extensively. And the lawyers are not going to suddenly agree with one another over the legal theories of the case.

Of course, it is still important to discuss some legal aspects of the case with the mediator during mediation. But that is a minor point compared to the primary purpose of mediation, which is to reach a deal. If you spend all your time arguing over why you are right and other party is wrong, then you will waste valuable time and resources in mediation. The other party will not agree with you, and the mediator is not there to decide if you are right. Better to focus on how much will it cost to end this lawsuit.

It's not always about the money. Keep that in mind as well. There are times when one party may want a non-monetary item to settle the lawsuit. This happens more often in trust and will disputes. For example, some family heirloom, family photographs, or a piece of furniture. These items could be something on which one party places a high value while the other does not. This means one person can receive a "valuable" (to them) item without the other party having to give up much of value.

The point is to keep an open mind. There are times when a creative solution will appear that allows everyone to walk away with something and, thereby, allowing the lawsuit to settle.

What Occurs at Mediation

Every mediator handles the process differently. But typically, mediation is conducted at the mediator's office. The parties are placed in separate rooms, and the mediator takes turns talking to each party by going from room to room.

The mediator will often start the day by talking to you about how mediation works and sharing some of the mediator's thoughts on the process. Some mediators will have the attorneys and parties sit in one room while they go over the mediation ground rules. Others will talk to each of the parties separately.

A good mediator will listen to you or your lawyer recite the facts of your case and make the relevant legal arguments. The mediator, however, is not there to make a decision. Rather, the mediator will expect one of the sides to start the process by making an offer to compromise the case. That initial offer will then be conveyed to the opposing party and a counter-offer will usually be made. This process of negotiation continues until either a settlement is reached or the mediation ends without settlement.

Many people describe this process as "shuttle diplomacy" because the mediator shuttles from room to room. Usually, before the mediator starts "shuttling," they will want to know something about you. A good mediator will ask you, the client, a few questions about your case, how you came to be in the lawsuit, and what your views of the case are up to this point. This is an important discussion because it is your chance to share your story with the mediator. The mediator needs this information for several reasons.

First, you and the mediator need to develop a relationship in a very short amount of time. You know going into mediation that the mediator is neutral, but you don't trust them right away. The mediator starts the process as a stranger to you. Yes, they are a professional, but we don't automatically trust professionals in this day and age. There was a time when that might have been true, but not now. And even if it were true now, the professional mediator still needs to develop trust with you if a deal is going to be reached.

Second, you need a chance to voice your side of the story. By talking with the mediator about your views of the facts, the case, and your desired result, you have a chance to vent. That's important because up to this point in your lawsuit you may feel that you have not had much of a chance to tell your side of the story. You need to stick up for yourself, voice your concerns, say what frustrates you about this case. Of course, your lawyer will speak up for you too, but don't be shy. Now's the time to get some of that story out to a neutral third party.

Third, the mediator is going to use some of your story when they are trying to convince the other party to settle. That does not mean the mediator will disclose anything you said in confidence (see the next section on mediation confidentiality), but it does mean some information will be used. And you want it to be used if the mediator can help you reach a deal.

For example, maybe the other party, or the other lawyer, does not know what happened to you, or what you have done prior to the lawsuit. And maybe that information would help the opposing party's lawyer see that a deal needs to be reached because the facts are not as good as they had thought they were.

A good mediator knows how to build trust, how to be direct, when to connect with you, and when to push you past resistance. Sometimes a mediator will tell you how bad your case is, and you'll think, "Is the mediator on the other person's side?" No, the mediator is on the side of settlement. Whatever bad things you hear about your case, the other side is hearing equally bad things from the mediator.

Professional mediators take their jobs seriously. They often are proud of the percentage of cases they have settled, and they want to settle your case too. A good mediator will have an idea of where the case should settle too. The mediator will not tell you that, at least not right away, but they can evaluate a case well and have probably seen a case just like yours many times before.

For these reasons, private mediations are typically more successful at reaching resolutions. The mediator is focused on your case, and only your case. The mediator has a strong desire to settle your case. And the mediator will stay with the mediation as long as it takes to settle. For instance, we have been at mediations that have lasted until well past midnight. Sometimes it takes a while, but a good mediator will get the job done.

That's not to say that every case will settle. Some certainly do not, but if a settlement is to be reached, a good mediator will find it and guide the parties to resolution.

Confidentiality

Under California's rules of evidence, anything said by a party at mediation is strictly confidential. The mediator is under a duty not to disclose anything you say to the other side unless you specifically grant the mediator permission to do so. Even if the mediator does disclose information to either party, that information is still confidential as between the parties and cannot be used for any purpose in the case afterward.

For example, one party may admit to something during the mediation process that is disclosed, with permission, to the other side. If a settlement is not reached, that admission could NOT be used for any purpose in the case, including trial, because anything said in an attempt to compromise a case is protected. And protected information cannot be used as evidence. This rule is meant to encourage parties to initiate settlement discussions in the hope of resolving the case—and without the penalty of having something said in furtherance of a settlement used against a party at a later date.

There's another aspect to confidentiality, and that is anything said between you and your lawyer at mediation is also confidential. Isn't this always the case when speaking with your lawyer? Yes, as between you and the outside world. Anything you discuss with your lawyer cannot be disclosed to anyone else without your permission. But the mediation confidentiality precludes even you from using conversations with your attorney for any later malpractice lawsuit against your attorney. This is different from any other attorney-client communications.

If your lawyer gives you advice, and then that advice is wrong, you may have a malpractice lawsuit against your lawyer. You can use the conversation you had with your lawyer as evidence in your malpractice lawsuit. But if you had a discussion with your lawyer at mediation, then you cannot use that discussion in any later malpractice lawsuit. In other words, the mediation privilege is so strong that even you can't use things said during the mediation to later sue your lawyer.

In fact, the California legislature will now require attorneys to have their clients sign an acknowledgement prior to their clients' agreeing to attend mediation. The acknowledgement required to be signed is as follows:

Mediation Disclosure Notification and Acknowledgment

To promote communication in mediation, California law generally makes mediation a confidential process. California's mediation confidentiality laws are laid out in Sections 703.5 and 1115 to 1129, inclusive, of the California Evidence Code. Those laws establish the confidentiality of mediation and limit the disclosure, admissibility, and a court's consideration of communications, writings, and conduct in connection with a mediation. In general, those laws mean the following:

- *All communications, negotiations, or settlement offers in the course of a mediation must remain confidential.*
- *Statements made and writings prepared in connection with a mediation are not admissible or subject to discovery or compelled disclosure in noncriminal proceedings.*
- *A mediator's report, opinion, recommendation, or finding about what occurred in a mediation may not be submitted to or considered by a court or another adjudicative body.*

A mediator cannot testify in any subsequent civil proceeding about any communication or conduct occurring at, or in connection with, a mediation.

This means that all communications between you and your attorney made in preparation for a mediation, or during a mediation, are confidential and cannot be disclosed or used (except in extremely limited circumstances), even if you later decide to sue your attorney for malpractice because of something that happens during the mediation.

I, _____, understand that, unless all participants agree otherwise, no oral or written communication made during a mediation, or in preparation for a mediation, including communications between me and my attorney, can be used as evidence in any subsequent noncriminal legal action including an action against my attorney for malpractice or an ethical violation.

NOTE: This disclosure and signed acknowledgment does not limit your attorney's potential liability to you for professional malpractice, or prevent you from (1) reporting any professional misconduct by your attorney to the State Bar of California or (2) cooperating with any disciplinary investigation or criminal prosecution of your attorney.

Dated: _____

Name of Client

Parties Must be Present

It is mandatory that you appear at mediation. The process only works if each party is present during the entire mediation. That means you must travel to the place of the mediation on the scheduled date, so you can meaningfully participate in the process. You'll be glad you did because it is impossible to appreciate the mediation process without being present.

Occasionally, a party will be given an exception from appearing. Usually that party must be available by telephone in the event an offer is made, or a possible resolution is reached. But you should make every effort to attend your mediation if possible.

How Long Does It Take? The Magic's in the Process

Stewart Albertson has a saying about mediations: "Nothing good happens until the sun goes down." Simply put, mediations take time. Mediation is a process. It is nearly impossible for parties to show up to a meeting and immediately agree on a settlement. Negotiations just don't work that way.

Think about grass growing, paint drying, bread dough rising with yeast ... it takes time. As we mentioned before, your lawsuit is confusing and slow, and your mediation is no different. You can't force grass to grow faster or bread to rise faster, and you certainly can't force mediation to end sooner. Prepare yourself for a long day at mediation.

Most mediations will last from four to eight hours, or longer, because it takes time to reach a resolution. In fact, time is the secret ingredient of mediations. Why? That may be beyond our expertise to answer. But from our observations it seems that people need time to lower their defenses and see the way to an acceptable resolution. As the day goes by people soften, they start to see the complexities of the lawsuit, the costs, the emotional strain. After a full day of mediation, a path to resolution often emerges.

In any event, your mediation will probably last much longer than you thought it would. It comes with the territory.

Agreement is Reached...

If the parties are able to reach a compromise, then the agreement is usually reduced to writing at the mediation by the parties' attorneys and then signed before anyone leaves. In some cases, especially in trust and will lawsuits, the settlement agreement will need to be approved by the court. If that occurs, then the parties would still sign the agreement before leaving, and then one of the parties would be responsible for drafting a petition to the court seeking approval of the settlement agreement.

The settlement agreement usually includes a full release of all claims by all parties, meaning that the lawsuit is done once and for all.

The written settlement agreement is the most important part of mediation because it will form the basis of the agreement between the parties going forward. The settlement agreement effectively replaces the lawsuit in terms of your legal rights. And since everything said at mediation is confidential, the written and signed settlement agreement is the only permissible evidence of the settlement terms. You are not allowed to tell the court what someone said at mediation to try to prove what the agreement is, or what the agreement should be in your view. All the mediation conversations are confidential and cannot be used in court. Instead, the written word becomes the sole basis of your agreement, and your legal rights, after mediation.

For this purpose, it pays to take as much time as possible to ensure the written agreement is clear. Keep in mind, you never have enough time to review and revise the written agreement at mediation. The agreement is usually drafted at the end of the day, everyone is tired, everyone just wants to go home. In a perfect world, the lawyers would take time the next day drafting and revising the agreement, but the parties must sign the agreement before leaving mediation because most deals will fall through if not signed at the time of mediation. As a result, mediation agreements are not given the time they fully need to be as clear as they could be. This is the chaotic part of mediation, and you should know in advance that no written settlement agreement is perfect.

However, within the time constraints you have in mediation, the written settlement agreement should be reviewed and revised as carefully as possible. Unfortunately, you can't think of every possible contingency that may arise when you draft the written agreement. You must do your best and also hope for the best. Most agreements work out as intended.

Agreement is NOT Reached...

If an agreement is not reached at the mediation, then the parties continue the lawsuit just as they did before going to mediation. That means discovery (such as depositions and written discovery) continues, and the case is prepared for trial in court where the final determination will be made either by a judge or jury, depending on the type of case you have.

Due to mediation confidentiality, none of the information you obtained during mediation can be used afterwards in court. However, that does not stop you from obtaining the same information from independent sources. For example, if you were shown a bank statement during mediation in an attempt to settle, you can't use the information you saw from that statement in court. But you can subpoena the bank and obtain a copy of that same bank statement for yourself. The information is out there somewhere, you just need to find it.

The exception would be statements from the opposing party. If the opposing party made a statement favorable to you or your case, you can't use that statement against them after mediation.

Change of Mind

There are times when parties wake up the morning after reaching a settlement at mediation and have buyer's remorse. They suddenly decide that the agreement was a bad deal and want to get out of it and continue the lawsuit.

Do yourself a favor, if you ever change your mind about a settlement after mediation, change your mind right back to settlement ... and fast! In most cases, it's just not possible to get out of a written settlement agreement after mediation.

Most agreements do not have a "get out of jail free" card. The agreements are written, signed, and enforceable in court. Also, many settlement agreements have an attorneys' fees clause that requires you to pay the other party's attorneys' fees if you challenge the settlement agreement in court and lose.

Further, courts favor settlements. If you go to court trying to overturn a written settlement agreement, the court will probably rule against you. The court wants you to settle. Courts have too many cases on their dockets as it is and not enough judges and court personnel to handle them all. As such, the court has a strong incentive to favor settlement.

In other words, learn to love your settlement agreement because, like it or not, you're stuck with it.

There are a few very limited circumstances where a settlement agreement may be overturned. And there are some settlement agreements that have "out" clauses. But these situations are rare. Chances are, your settlement agreement is here to stay.

On Costs

Mediations vary in cost depending on whom you use as a mediator. Private attorneys who offer mediation services usually are the lowest cost option at around $500 per hour, with a four-hour minimum (that's a minimum of $1,500 for the mediation session). The parties usually split the cost of the mediator equally. Whereas retired judges with a good reputation for settling cases can cost between $8,000 to $10,000 per day, with each party paying half of that amount (assuming you have two parties to the lawsuit).

There are times when the parties may agree to a different payment allocation. For example, if three equal trust beneficiaries are fighting over a trust estate, they may agree to have the trust pay for the mediation, rather than each party paying from their own pocket. The parties can vary the payment allocation any way they choose, if they can agree to it. Otherwise, the mediation fees are borne equally by each party.

The cost of the mediator is one of the big downsides of private mediation. The result tends to be better than an MSC, but it comes at a price. And that price can increase substantially depending on whom you use as a mediator. Whether the costs are worth it or not depends on the value of your case. If you are suing over millions, then maybe a fee of $10,000 is no big deal. If, however, you are suing over $50,000, then a $10,000 fee is hard to justify. You need to match the mediator to the case. That means considering the price and complexity of the issues involved in your lawsuit. The simpler, less expensive cases can use a less expensive mediator.

Finally, some California counties have low-cost mediation options that offer different types of mediation services at differing rate schedules depending on the type of case and whether it is a court referral. In these types of mediations, you typically do not have a choice of mediator, but the costs can be substantially lower. In some cases, you may be given two to three hours for free. It pays to check out the settlement options offered by your local court. They are often changing available options and trying new ideas, so see what you can find. This is especially important for smaller cases where the costs of mediation have to be more seriously considered.

In addition to the cost of the mediator, there are the attorneys' fees in preparing the mediation brief (which gives the mediator an understanding of your side of the case) and attorneys' fees for attending the mediation. These are necessary costs for any mediation, regardless of how expensive the mediator is.

Mediations- How Many?

Most cases will only have one mediation because a majority of cases settle at the first mediation. For those cases that do not settle, parties are able to attend additional mediations if they are willing to incur the additional cost and expense of doing so—although most cases do not have more than one mediation session. There is no limit to the number of mediations you can have in a single case, so you can do dozens of mediations if you so desire (believe us, no one should desire that!).

At times, cases can even settle after an unsuccessful mediation on the same, or similar, terms and conditions that were worked out at the mediation session. Many mediators will check in with the parties after mediation to determine if a settlement can be reached. As mentioned before, mediators take their settlement percentages seriously. If the mediator believes they can settle a case even after mediation, they will do so in many cases. Alternatively, we have had cases where one party reaches out to the mediator after an unsuccessful mediation and asks the mediator to convey an offer to the opposing party. Anything can happen, so keep your eyes and ears open for possible settlement discussions as your case progresses. Flexibility is key to resolving your case during the settlement phase. If a good offer presents itself to you, take it.

Mediation and Arbitration: The Difference

Do not confuse arbitration with mediation. They are two different procedures. Mediation is an informal meeting of the parties with a neutral mediator who tries to reach a voluntary compromise.

Arbitration is like a mini-trial where an arbitrator makes a binding decision in your case. In other words, arbitration replaces your right to a trial in court with either a judge or jury (not all lawsuits are entitled to juries—such as probate, trust, and will cases).

Arbitrators are allowed to make decisions without the rules of evidence, they oftentimes limit the amount of discovery that can be done (thereby impeding your ability to obtain evidence), and their decisions cannot be appealed in court. As a result, we do not favor arbitrations. But there are times when arbitrations are required. If that is the case in your matter, your lawyer will inform you of this.

Unlike mediation, which is an informal settlement discussion that takes place with a neutral third party, an arbitration is a more formal procedure to resolve a case. Arbitration is like a mini-trial that uses some, but not all, of the rules of evidence typically used in court. An arbitration is presided over by anywhere from one to three arbitrators (usually lawyers or retired judges) who hear evidence on the case and then make a forced decision. In a majority of cases, an arbitrator's decision is binding and must be followed by the parties. This is a forced decision of the case rather than a voluntary compromise between the parties. There can be non-binding arbitration, where the arbitrator's decision is subject to review by the court, but that is a less common procedure.

Some of the more common contracts that include arbitration provisions are business contracts, standard residential real estate contracts (including listing agreements), title insurance policies, and other types of insurance policies, health insurance policies, and some employment agreements. In these instances, the arbitration process is the only method by which a dispute can be decided, and any lawsuit filed in court is subject to removal to arbitration upon motion filed by any one of the parties.

Section 4 Brief

Your case will settle before trial. With 97% of civil cases settling before trial, you have little chance of resolving your case any other way. Once you pay your attorneys' fees and costs for a few months, not to mention enduring emotional turmoil, you will desire a settlement. And that's fine because you can achieve great results in settlement if you approach them properly. By being flexible, persistent, and resilient, you can prepare yourself to successfully navigate the mediation/settlement phase of your case.

For those cases that do not settle, we now visit some pretrial issues you should be aware of.

Section 5

Other Pretrial Concerns

There are two more considerations before we move to the trial phase. Those are (1) termination motions, namely summary judgment and summary adjudication, and (2) expert witnesses. Section 5 covers both.

YOUR LAWSUIT • 111

CHAPTER 13

Terminating Motions

Wouldn't it be great to win your case without having to spend money for a full-blown trial in front of a jury or judge? That's where terminating motions come into play. Terminating motions refer to certain motions that allow the court to make a final decision on your case without the need for a trial. The two terminating motions we focus on in this chapter are summary judgments and summary adjudications.

In some cases, one of the parties may believe that they are entitled to a decision in their favor before trial because there is not enough evidence to decide against them. The procedure used to ask the court to decide in a party's favor before trial is called a "summary judgment" if it's for a decision that ends the entire case, or a "summary adjudication" if it's for a decision that ends only part of a case. The reason these motions are referred to as "summary" is that they take place before trial, and if you win the motion, will obviate the need for a trial.

A summary judgment, referred to as "MSJ," which stands for "motion for summary judgment," and a summary adjudication, or "MSA," which stands for "motion for summary adjudication," are generally not favored by the court. Remember, our legal system is based on due process of law. And due process requires that each party be given an equal and fair chance to present admissible evidence at trial. Deciding the case, or some part of the case, without a trial is unfair, except in limited circumstances. As such, MSJs and MSAs are rarely granted by the court.

When Would a Court Grant it?

MSJs and MSAs are used in cases where the evidence, even if viewed in a light most favorable to the other party, is not sufficient to support the result requested. In the legal world we say there must be no triable issue of fact in order for the court to grant an MSJ or MSA. But what does "triable issue of fact" mean?

Think of the jury's role in a trial. The jury is empowered to hear the evidence and decide the truth. The jury decides which facts are true and which facts are false. Based on the jury's view of the facts, the jury then decides who wins and who loses. The same is true for a bench trial where a judge decides the facts, instead of a jury. Either way, there is a trier of facts—a person or persons who are entitled to decide the truth versus the falsities.

But what if there are no facts for which truth or falsity need be determined? For example, in our hypothetical contract dispute with Bob, if Bob admits there is a written contract and has no defense to why it should not be enforced, then there are no facts to decide. We have the contract, we know the terms, we know what Bob paid so far and what Bob did not pay, and there are no other facts required to rule on the case. If Bob is not contesting these facts, then Bob really has nothing to say come time of trial as to why the contract should not be enforced. As a result, the court can simply grant your MSJ, rule that the contract is binding and enforceable, and issue a judgment against Bob for the remaining contract payments.

If, however, Bob's defense is that you breached the contract first by taking his car back from him, which you deny doing, then we have some facts that need deciding. Is Bob telling the truth or are you? Only a jury can decide that question.

When facts need to be decided in order to make a legal ruling on a case, then a trial must happen. But when the facts are not disputed, or one side has no facts to support their claims or defenses, then a trial is simply not necessary. The law can be applied, and the jury can be saved for another case.

Bringing an MSJ or MSA is hard work. Both types of motions require compliance with a technical procedure. And the motions take time to draft and also require various supporting documents. It is never an easy undertaking to bring an MSJ or MSA, but it may be worthwhile depending on the type of case you have. Remember that courts do not favor these types of motions, so you must provide overwhelming arguments and information to ensure you have a chance of winning.

While such motions are not routinely granted, they must be taken seriously because losing an MSJ or MSA would mean the end of a case before trial. You want to be sure the court understands why you are entitled to a trial on the merits of the case. And you certainly do not want to lose the case before trial if you can avoid doing so. Filing or opposing an MSJ adds additional time and expense to any lawsuit.

If your case survives a terminating motion, then you need to start preparing for trial. In most cases, that means it's time to bring in the experts.

CHAPTER 14

Expert Witnesses

The wonderful world of expert witnesses … If you have not hired an expert witness before, then you are in for a treat. Experts are a necessary part of many lawsuits, but they don't come cheaply. Qualified experts can cost tens of thousands, or hundreds of thousands, of dollars. In most cases, the expert is worth every penny. But be fore-warned, hiring and using expert witnesses will be a consider-able expense in your lawsuit.

Why do you need experts? Experts help in many ways. Experts allow you to present to the judge or jury opinions, cir-cumstances, recreations, medical diagnoses, and other critical case information that normal (non-expert) witnesses cannot.

Normal witnesses, referred to as "fact witnesses" or "per-cipient witnesses," are only allowed to testify about infor-mation for which they have personal knowledge. For example, if I were standing on a street corner, I saw a red light, and then I saw a car speed through the red light and hit another car, I could testify to those facts because I witnessed them myself.

Suppose now that I was not standing on that street corner, and no one saw the car accident. Instead, you want to recreate the accident using the skid marks on the road, the damage caused to the car, and all the other information that would seem to indicate what had occurred. Well, you can't testify to all that because you probably don't have the expert knowledge to give that opinion. And no one actually saw the crash happening in real time—so there are no fact witnesses to recreate the accident. What you need is an accident reconstruction expert, someone who has the proper education and experience to piece together the information obtained after the crash and, thereby, recreate the accident. This is an expert opinion.

The only way to introduce evidence of the crash recreation is through the testimony of an expert witness. The same is true for things like medical diagnoses. A medical expert can read medical files, take all the medical information contained in those files, and then give an expert opinion on the diagnosis of the patient. This expert opinion is allowed even though the expert did not personally observe the facts contained in the medical records.

Some experts focus on financial information. For example, forensic accountants are often needed to trace assets in fraud lawsuits. At Albertson & Davidson, LLP, we have handled many trust or will cases where a trustee or executor mishandled or embezzled money. A forensic accountant can review the financial records, trace the money, and help build a case for what occurred with the finances.

Experts are allowed to review all relevant documentation and other information, and then create an expert opinion based on that information. During trial, the expert will then testify to their expert opinion.

Anytime you have an expert witness, you can bet the other side will have a similar expert. Your expert will say one thing, and the opposing expert will say the opposite. This is what we call the battle of the experts. For example, in a lack of capacity case where you are trying to overturn a trust or will, your expert will say the decedent, meaning the deceased person, lacked capacity to create the document. The opposing party's expert will say the decedent had capacity to create the document. Who wins? That's up to the judge or jury to decide.

The interesting thing about experts is that the jury (or the judge if you have a bench trial) can choose to believe the expert, reject the expert, or anything in between. Just because the witness is an expert does not mean the jury must believe their testimony. Ultimately, the jury will decide which expert to believe, or they may choose to ignore them all. This is another chaotic, and confusing, aspect of your lawsuit. The better you understand the possible outcomes of hiring an expert, the better you can handle the unexpected.

That may be the irony of experts, you can use them, you will pay them, but they may never be believed by the jury. Unfortunately, experts are still a necessary part of your lawsuit. Why?

First, there is some information a jury will never hear without the testimony of an expert witness. For example, in the case of medical records there are many diagnoses in the records that cannot be introduced at trial because they are hearsay (we'll talk about hearsay more in chapter 15). But an expert can read those hearsay medical records, form their own opinion, and then testify to that opinion in court. The expert is not allowed to read or repeat the information from the medical records verbatim, but the expert can state their opinion. For example, if a patient is diagnosed with dementia a year ago, the expert can testify that in their opinion the patient was suffering from dementia and, thereby, did not have legal capacity to create a will. That's a valuable advantage for any lawsuit.

Second, a good expert is believable, will be believed and accepted by the jury, and will, therefore, be valuable to your case. You cannot underestimate the value of a good expert witness who connects with the jury, provides believable opinions, and provides helpful information about the case. At Albertson & Davidson, LLP, we have hired more expert witnesses than we can count. Our experience helps us determine the great experts (who are likely to be believed come time of trial) from the not-so-great experts. That guidance can be crucial if you wish to increase the success of your case.

Third, you have no other option. If you want to present evidence of something complex, such as an accident recreation, you have no choice but to use an expert. The same is true for medical diagnoses, forensic accounting, engineering issues, the list goes on and on. There are many complex things in this world that are issues in lawsuits; thus, experts are needed.

Section 5 Brief

There are many more pretrial considerations than can be included in this book, but terminating motions and experts are the most important aspects of your lawsuit prior to trial.

Next, it's time for the main event: trial.

Section 6

The Trial Phase

This is the big show. Not many cases make it to trial because they settle beforehand. And some cases will settle in the middle of trial. But for those cases that can only be resolved by trial, the time has come to produce your evidence. This final section covers the ins and outs of trials and appeals. For readers involved in trust or will contests, there's a chapter dedicated to the no-contest clause.

CHAPTER 15

Trial Time

Trial is the point in the process where evidence is presented to the court and a decision is made by the judge or jury. In probate matters, which is just about anything filed in probate court including trust matters, a judge will decide your case. In civil matters, either party may request a jury trial. If neither party request a jury trial, or if both parties agree, then a judge will hear and decide the case.

Trials are usually longer than you think they will be or should be. And the trial process can take time to begin because of certain actions the parties take with things like pretrial motions. Let's go over some trial basics and then discuss the most important aspects of trial.

What a Trial Is

A trial is meant to be an orderly process where each side is given a fair chance to fully present evidence to the court. Either a judge or jury will hear testimony and then make a decision on who is right and who is wrong.

Judges have wide discretion on how a trial proceeds. And every judge is different in terms of the process they want to use, the expectations they have of the lawyers and parties, and the amount of time they will allow for each side to make their case. Judges have the right to set the ground rules in their own courtroom for every aspect of the trial process. That does not mean the judge can change the law or take away your right to a jury, but when it comes to the procedures and process to be used for trial, the judge is king.

What a Trial Isn't

Trial is not a time for everyone to say everything they think about the case. In other words, the testimony and documents you are allowed to use at trial are limited. The rules of evidence place rules on the information that is used versus the information that is not used. If your information (documents and witnesses) doesn't conform to the rules of evidence, then it cannot be used at trial. Expect to find a section in this chapter dedicated to evidence.

Trial also is not a process where the judge will do any independent research into the facts of your case. The judge or jury is only there to make a decision on the facts they are provided by the parties, not to conduct an independent investigation. In fact, it is improper for the jury to look up information independently during trial.

And finally, trial is not meant to reach an entirely fair result in every case. There are times when the law is unfair. The law is not unfair by design, but the law can be unfair by application. For example, let's say you were hurt in an accident, and you had the right to sue a big company to pay for your damages, but you failed to file your lawsuit until one day after the statute of limitations deadline, and, therefore, you cannot recover anything. We, as people, can probably agree that is unfair. A person was hurt, the law allows them to be paid damages for their harms and losses, and yet that person receives nothing. But the law set a deadline by which a lawsuit must be filed; since that deadline was violated, the results are legal, but unfair.

This is just one example of an unfair result. There could be any number of scenarios where a decision made by a jury or judge is legal, but unfair. We hope that in most cases the judgment is both fair and legal, but the judge or jury does not always have the ability to create a fair result because they are required to follow the law too.

The point here is to be prepared for an unfair outcome. Trial is chaotic and unpredictable—failure is always an option at trial. If your lawsuit is a lesson in flexibility, persistence, and resilience, then your trial is the final exam. Even in cases where the judge or jury wants to fashion a fair result, they may not be able to do so because of the legal constraints under which they operate. Keep that in mind as you are heading into trial.

Pretrial Motions

Before the trial can really begin, the parties often must deal with various pretrial motions. The most common example of a pretrial motion is the motion *in limine*. *Limine* is Latin for "at the threshold," referring to a motion before trial begins. Motions *in limine* are brought to prevent certain evidence from being seen or heard by the jury.

Normally, a party is allowed to ask any questions they like of a witness. The opposing party can voice an objection at the time of questioning, and the judge will either sustain or overrule the objection. But there are times when even asking a question could be problematic even if the judge sustains an objection to the question.

For example, if we were to ask a witness, "When did you first start selling cocaine for a living?" the other side may have a legitimate objection to that question. Maybe the question is not relevant to the lawsuit because we are suing for breach of a real estate contract that has nothing to do with selling cocaine (or any other drugs for that matter). The judge will likely sustain the objection and prevent us from receiving an answer to that question. But you can bet that the question will attract the attention of the jury, even if the judge says the question cannot be answered. To prevent the jury from hearing this question, the opposing party would bring a motion *in limine* asking the judge to order us not to ask the question in the first place.

"You can't un-ring the bell" is a common saying for motions *in limine*. Once we ask a witness about their cocaine-selling past, the jury can't un-hear that question. It naturally will taint that witness and cause the jury to believe the witness is not to be trusted. The judge can sustain the objection and prevent the witness from answering the question, but the damage is already done.

Motions *in limine* must be brought before trial begins. Some courts require the motions to be filed a few weeks before trial, and others will receive the motions on the first day the parties meet to start the trial process. How do you know what an opposing attorney will ask at trial? Depositions, of course. In fact, that is one of the primary reasons to take depositions: so you have advance notice of problematic questions and answers.

In many cases, both parties will bring a number of motions *in limine*, some of which are granted while others are not. Every judge has a different view on the proper use of motions *in limine*, but they generally should only be used to prevent damage that cannot be repaired once the jury hears bad information.

Case In Chief

Since each side is given a fair chance to present evidence at trial, each side has their own case to present. But you can't present both sides of a case at the same time. So one party goes first, and then the other party goes second.

Usually the plaintiff or petitioner goes first—whoever has the burden of proof is first up. And each side has a "case in chief," meaning their presentation of the case. If you are first up, then you present your case in chief—meaning your list of witnesses and documents that you want the judge or jury to consider. During your case in chief, the other side can cross-examine your witnesses, but they cannot call their own witnesses yet. That will come later when they put on their case in chief.

This system provides an orderly presentation of witnesses and documents. The first side is allowed to bring all witnesses and documents it wants to present to the court, and the opposing side cross-examines, but does not call additional witnesses and does not introduce additional documents. Once the first side is done, then the second party is allowed to call their list of witnesses and documents, while the first party does the cross-examination.

There are times when witness or document may be taken out of order for timing reasons. The court has the power to do so when necessary or when requested and agreed to by the parties. You may hear an attorney say they have no questions for a particular witness, but they reserve the right to recall the witness to the stand during their case in chief. Or the judge may ask if a witness can be excused, and an attorney will say no because the witness is needed for their case in chief. Since each side has the right to put on their own case, in their own way, any witness can be recalled at a later time, provided that they are not first excused as a witness. Once the judge excuses the witness, then the witness is no longer under an obligation to appear and give testimony. So your lawyer should be careful when agreeing to excuse a witness.

Jury Selection

There are entire books written about jury selection. This is not one of them. The only point we would like to make about jury selection is that it is more art than science. There are big companies that hire expensive jury consultants to pick the perfect jury. And every trial lawyer seems to have their own approach on how to properly pick a good jury.

For you, the party to the lawsuit, it is important to know that jury instruction can take a long time. The process starts with the judge asking some standard questions of the jurors to determine if anyone has a conflict of interest that would preclude them from serving on the jury. For example, if someone is a friend or relative of one of the parties, then that person would be excluded from serving.

The parties will each be given a set amount of time by the judge to question the jury. This is called *voire dire*. The purpose of *voire dire* is to give each attorney a chance to probe the potential jurors to ensure they will be fair and follow the law. If a juror expresses a view to be not fair, or refuses to follow the law, then that juror will not serve on the jury. The judge will excuse the juror "for cause," meaning they do not meet the requirements for service on that jury.

Each side is also given preemptory challenges, meaning they can ask the court to excuse any juror for any reason, or no reason, at all.

Once the jury answers the judge's questions and each of the parties' questions, and all the "for cause" and "preemptory" challenges are finished, the jury is seated. The jury usually consists of twelve people, plus two alternates.

For civil cases the jury does not have to return a unanimous result. The jury only needs nine out of the twelve to agree on the outcome of the case. That is different from the standard in criminal cases where all twelve jurors must agree on the decision.

Opening Statement

After the jury is seated, each party is then given a chance to present an opening statement. Opening statements are rather odd in that you, or your lawyer if you have one, are not supposed to present any arguments. You are only supposed to lay out what the evidence will show in the upcoming trial. Why no argument? Mainly because that is the purpose of closing argument. After all the testimony and evidence is heard by the court, then the parties are allowed to argue to the jury what the evidence establishes. Sound confusing? It is, but bear this in mind and you will better understand why the opening statement is not exactly what you were hoping for.

This is an age-old rule and many judges will allow some argument to creep into opening statements, but not much. What you should know is that the rules limit what you or your lawyer can say during opening statements; whereas, the rules are far more liberal on what can be said and argued during closing statements.

Evidence

Evidence must set foundation (authenticate), not be hearsay or fall within a hearsay exception, and be relevant to the issues at trial.

The number one goal of the evidence code is to ensure the use of credible information during trial. The cornerstone of evidence is authentication. If you are going to use a bank statement as evidence, for example, the court must ensure that document is really a bank statement created by the bank. Obviously, we don't want people creating false documents. The evidence code provides a procedure for authenticating documents.

The rules contained under the evidence code are also meant to promote fairness and prevent undue prejudice against a party. What does all that mean? All evidence is prejudicial against one party or the other. When a witness testifies that they saw someone run a red light, that testimony is prejudicial to the person who ran the red light. But if that evidence is relevant to the case, then it is allowed to be used at trial.

If, however, a witness wants to testify that they saw the defendant run a red light five years ago, and so it must stand to reason that the defendant ran a red light last year when the accident related to the lawsuit occurred, that would not be allowed at trial. The fact that someone ran a red light once five years ago is not relevant to the current accident lawsuit, and is not allowed to show a pattern of running red lights, and such testimony would be unfairly prejudicial to the defendant. In other words, we want evidence that is relevant and fair to be used in the current lawsuit, but not evidence that is too far removed from the issues involved in the current lawsuit.

Another example is past criminal actions. If you are suing someone for breach of trust, you probably will not be able to use their past criminal conviction for a DUI against them. In most cases, it would be unfairly prejudicial to suggest that someone should lose a contract case just because they have a past conviction for a DUI. That can change, however, if the DUI issued is directly relevant to the current lawsuit. For example, if a truck driver is hired by a company, and the driver lied on their application about having a past DUI, then evidence of the past DUI conviction would be relevant to the lawsuit.

The evidence code is meant to limit the information that can be used at trial in an effort to ensure a more fair, and hopefully accurate, evidentiary record. Since only admissible evidence can be considered by the jury or judge, it is important to have a fair playing field for allowing evidence into trial. We wouldn't want a system where trials were decided based on smear campaigns rather than credible facts and witnesses demonstrating relevant information. This isn't politics after all—the court system has standards!

Hearsay

Hearsay is part of the evidence code, but we want to discuss it separately because it can be a confusing topic—both for lawyers and laypersons. Hearsay is an evidentiary rule that you have probably heard before, but you may not know, or understand, what the term means. In short, hearsay refers to anything said or written outside of court. In legal terms, we call anything said or written outside of court as an "out-of-court statement." For example, if I tell you a stoplight was red when a car ran through it, that is an out-of-court statement. When a party attempts to use an out-of-court statement or writing at trial, the other side will object based on hearsay (out-of-court statements cannot be used to prove a fact in court).

The reason the law disfavors hearsay testimony is our system is based on due process. And due process requires fairness, which includes giving each party an equal opportunity to examine, and cross-examine, every witness. You are supposed to be given a fair chance to question your accusers in court before a judge and jury. Hearsay takes away that right. Let's look at an example to better demonstrate hearsay.

Let's say Bob was standing on a street corner and saw Tom drive through an intersection, running a red light. Bob saw the light, saw the car run the red light, and then saw the resulting accident. After the accident occurred, Ida walked out of a store (having seen nothing of the accident) and asked Bob, "What happened here?" Bob explained that Tom ran the red light and caused and accident.

At trial the plaintiff would want Bob to testify to what Bob saw to help prove that Tom was negligent and should be held accountable for the damages incurred. But the plaintiff can't find Bob anywhere. So, instead, the plaintiff asks Ida to come to court and testify to what Bob told her about the accident. Ida agrees to do so and is called to the witness stand. The plaintiff's lawyer asks Ida, "What did Bob tell you about the accident?" The defendant objects based on hearsay. Will the court agree?

Yes. This is a classic example of hearsay evidence. Ida cannot testify to what Bob told her about the accident because that was an out-of-court statement. In other words, the plaintiff has the wrong witness on the stand. Ida cannot be cross-examined by the defendant about where Ida was standing, what Ida saw, the color of the car Ida saw, and whether Ida was sure it was really Tom. Ida doesn't know any of this because Ida didn't witness the accident. Bob could answer those questions because he was the one who witnessed the whole thing.

That essentially is hearsay. If you are asking a witness what someone other than the witness said, then you probably are asking about hearsay information. The same is true for documents, as all documents are statements made by someone, somewhere, outside of court.

Yet documents and many other hearsay statements are used in trials every day, how is that possible? That brings us to the more than twenty-two exceptions to the hearsay rule. Confusion is abundant when it comes to hearsay and its exceptions. Your job, or your lawyer's job, is to figure out which hearsay exception applies to each piece of evidence you want to use. Experience counts when wading through these issues.

For example, bank statements are hearsay because they are prepared by the bank outside of court. Yet, one of the biggest exceptions to the hearsay rule is for business records.

If you have the custodian of records declare under penalty of perjury that the documents are authentic and that they were prepared in the ordinary course of business, then you can use those records in court. You have to follow the rules on how to introduce that type of evidence, but the point being the evidence can be used—there is a way.

What you really need to know about evidence is that you must follow the rules. Not everything you think relevant can, or will, be used at trial. But if you prepare properly and follow the evidence code, you can have a substantial amount of your evidence used at trial.

Direct and Cross-Exam

There is a lot more that goes into trials than just the witnesses and documents. Each of the parties' attorneys has a fair chance to examine and cross-examine witnesses. This is a big part of trial and the one part that most people can identify by watching movies or television (with such lines as "You can't handle the truth!").

Most witness examinations are routine and rather boring. Rarely is the time when a witness gives a shocking answer or suddenly admits the truth due to the cunning questions of the lawyers. Every lawyer would like to think that they can achieve the perfect testimony from a witness by asking the right questions, in the right sequence. That's not typically the case.

What do you need to know about witness examination? First, it's not so easy. It can be much more difficult to conduct a direct exam and cross-exam than you think. As with everything at trial, there are rules you must follow when conducting witness examination.

For instance, on direct examination of a witness you are not allowed to ask leading questions. Leading questions are those that suggest the answer and typically only require a yes or no answer. "Isn't it true that you own a green Cadillac?" is a leading question. Whereas asking, "What type of car do you own?" is not a leading question because the answer is not contained in the question itself.

Prohibiting leading questions on direct examination can make it difficult to guide the witness. If you ask a witness, "Tell me about the night of January 1, 2018," they may not know what specifically you want to hear. You may prepare the witness beforehand, but that doesn't always help. Being a trial witness is stressful and can be overwhelming to many. Any preparation is often forgotten the moment a witness sits in the witness stand. As such, there is certainly an art to asking good questions in order to obtain helpful answers.

Cross-examination is different because you can use leading questions. But cross-examination can also be more difficult because you have a hostile witness who does not want to cooperate with you … usually.

The point to all of this is to let you know that examination is not as easy as it looks in the movies and television. This discussion is not meant to teach you how to conduct a proper examination (that's the topic of another book). These are simply some basics, so you can know what to expect and lessen any potential confusion before you head into trial with your lawyer.

Multi-Day Trials

Some trials cannot be completed within a single day. When trials require more than one day, they can either continue on consecutive days … or not. There are many times when the court is not available on consecutive days—especially in bench trials where the judge is deciding your case. In that instance, the trial may be continued over several weeks or even months, which means you will have large breaks in between trial days.

Many people are surprised when this occurs because they think the court conducts consecutive-day trials. But courts are busy places where they have far more cases than judges and court personnel to handle them. In fact, it is quite common for the court to schedule three to six cases for trial at the same time. Of course, a court cannot hear more than one trial at a time, but the court double- or triple-books the trial calendar anyway because most cases will either settle or be postponed for some reason or another.

While courts try to schedule consecutive trial dates, it's not always possible. If your trial is not conducted over consecutive days, then you may find it spread out over a few weeks, with a few days of trial each week.

You should be prepared for this possibility in your case. And if this does occur, try to make your schedule as available as possible to accommodate the next trial day.

Your Role and Obligation

As a party to the lawsuit you have the right to be present during trial. You may also have the obligation to testify if you are called to testify as a witness by your attorney or by the opposing attorney. All your friends and family can also be present during trial unless they are witnesses. Those testifying as witnesses may be excluded from the courtroom during trial to prevent them from hearing the testimony of others.

Otherwise, every trial (with limited exceptions) is open to the public. Anyone, and everyone, is allowed to sit in the chairs behind the short wall that separates the parties from the rest of the courtroom and watch the case unfold. Of course, few people choose to do so on most cases (unless you happen to be a celebrity), but the invitation is open all the same.

Most likely you are not going to do much talking or explaining in your case. Trials are formal affairs. The only time you will talk is when you are asked a question on the witness stand. The attorneys, and the judge, are all allowed to ask questions of you. Once the questions are asked, you sit down and the trial continues with other witnesses.

You can talk to your attorney during trial by passing notes, and you can discuss issues during breaks, but you won't be allowed to contribute while trial is underway. This is where you should let your attorney do their job for you. You spent a great deal of time, money, and emotion reaching this point. It's time to let the case be tried by the person, or people, you hired to do so.

Closing Argument

This is where the trial all comes together. All the evidence has been heard, all the documents are before the court (if they survived the rules of the evidence code), and it's time to make your pitch. Closing is the first chance your lawyer really has to argue your case. Almost anything goes in a closing argument. As already mentioned, it is much more broad and liberal than the opening statement.

In particular, your lawyer will want to connect the law with the facts. For example, if you have a lawsuit where you must prove someone's lack of capacity, then your lawyer will discuss the elements for their lacking of capacity, such as not knowing the type of property they own, with the testimony and documents that supported that element.

This is a time to discuss the equities of your case as well. Those of the fairness issues that so often are the focus of client's thoughts even though they rarely meet the legal requirements for your lawsuit. But the jury or judge is composed of people, and people like fairness in our society. In other words, it's not just about the law in a closing argument, it is about the underlying principle that supports your desired result. Now is the time to bring this up to the jury and take your best shot at reaching a fair result.

There is one caveat to closing arguments: you cannot violate the Golden Rule. You remember the Golden Rule, "Do unto others as you would have them do unto you"? That same concept applies to the closing argument. You cannot make an argument that asks a juror to determine what they would like to receive in damages if they were a party to the lawsuit. In other words, you cannot make an argument where you ask the jurors to put themselves in a party's position because it then would make their decision based on personal interests.

Of course, lawyers often play close to the line because we do want the jurors to be the "conscience of the community." Juries do set the bar as to what is, and what is not, acceptable in our society—they just happen to act one case at a time. But you still must be careful not to cross the line and ask the jury to do unto you what they would want done unto them.

Settlement During Trial

Just because your trial started does not mean your case can never settle. There are many instances where cases settle during trial. Sometimes it occurs before jury selection, after jury selection, after opening statements, after certain witnesses are questioned—you just never know.

You should be prepared to talk, however, because settlement opportunities could still arise. Also, many judges will work with the parties to reach a settlement before trial commences. You may have already attended a mediation, several mediations, or even MSCs, but the time is still ripe for further settlement talks.

The Big Decision

After all is said and done, and argued, the judge or jury will make a decision. Jury decisions are read out in the courtroom just like you see in the movies. Judge decisions are often issued in writing a few months after a trial concludes. Either way, the jury or judge decision will be the final determination of your case. Well, this is most likely true (see the next chapter on appeals).

Ultimately, the jury or judge decision will be reduced to a judgment (or order if you filed a petition in probate court) that will be enforceable under the law.

Post-Trial Motions

Once the trial is over, a party may bring a motion trying to set aside the jury's decision. This is hard to do and often fails, but there are limited circumstances where a judgment can be entered by the court that contradicts a jury's decision.

With a bench trial, the parties at times will request a written statement of decision. This means that the court, or one of the parties, will draft the reasoning behind the court's decision. This could be useful later if you plan to appeal your case. The appellate court has a hard time overturning a case where it does not know the legal grounds on which the case was decided.

In any event, just because the trial is over does not necessarily mean the work is over. There can still be a lot to do, either to challenge the decision, set the reasoning for the decision, or prepare to appeal the decision.

Trials are usually a winner-take-all proposition. As a result, parties often will seek to appeal the trial court's decision after trial. Next, we discuss some basic aspects of appeals.

CHAPTER 16

Appeals

So you want to appeal your lawsuit after trial? You should know that you are not entitled to a whole new trial in most cases. The appellate court has a strong bias to confirm the trial court's result.

In the normal world of civil lawsuits, the rules for when you must appeal are fairly easy to maneuver because it is based on the date the final judgment is approved by the court.

In trust and will lawsuits, however, there can be multiple petitions filed, each with their own order or judgment, and interim orders entered along the way. Knowing when and how to appeal can be tricky. And missing an appeal deadline stops you from ever seeking review of that order.

Luckily the California Probate Code provides a set of rules for appealing orders on trust, will (probate), conservatorship, and guardianship matters. The rules are found at Probate Code section 1300 to 1312.

For example, Section 1300 states that an appeal can be taken from the making of, or refusal to make, any of the following orders:

(a) Directing, authorizing, approving, or confirming the sale, lease, encumbrance, grant of an option, purchase, conveyance, or exchange of property.

(b) Settling an account of a fiduciary.

(c) Authorizing, instructing, or directing a fiduciary, or approving or confirming the acts of a fiduciary.

(d) Directing or allowing payment of a debt, claim, or cost.

(e) Fixing, authorizing, allowing, or directing payment of compensation or expenses of an attorney.

(f) Fixing, directing, authorizing, or allowing payment of the compensation or expenses of a fiduciary.

(g) Surcharging, removing, or discharging a fiduciary.

(h) Transferring the property of the estate to a fiduciary in another jurisdiction.

(i) Allowing or denying a petition of the fiduciary to resign.

(j) Discharging a surety on the bond of a fiduciary.

(k) Adjudicating the merits of a claim made under Section 850.

The code goes on to state specific rules for trust, probate, conservatorship, and guardianship actions.

This list is helpful to determine when an order becomes "final." For example, an order confirming the sale of real estate will be final as to that sale, but the overall probate case may still be ongoing. Normally, an entire lawsuit must be complete before appealing. But under Section 1300, you have the right to appeal the final sale order even while the probate continues.

This is good and bad. On the good side, it allows you to apply for an appeal earlier than you normally would do so. On the bad side, it sets the timeline to appeal in motion before the entire case is over, so you have to file your notice of appeal and go through the motions earlier than you normally would.

Chances for Success

Appealing a trial court's decision after trial is not so easy. That is true of nearly all civil cases actually—appellate review is rather limited in scope and, therefore, rarely results in overturning a trial court's decision. In fact, the law states that an appeal court is not supposed to re-try the case or re-decide the facts. The appellate court will only take action if the trial court abused its power, or the trial court ruling was based on no evidence. Even then, the appellate court will not re-try the case; it will simply send the case back to the trial court for another decision. In most cases, whatever facts were found to be true by the trial court will also be considered true by the appellate court.

The one exception is purely legal rules. The appellate court can make a new decision on a legal rule without regard to the trial court's decision. A pure legal ruling is any decision that relates to an interpretation of the law. For example, does a trust giving all assets to the elder's children apply to a child who was adopted by the elder after age eighteen? There are legal rules that determine when an adopted child can inherit and the age by which the adoption must take place. Answering this question is based solely on interpreting the law; thus, it's a purely legal question.

The mistake most people make about appeals is to think the appellate court will have a new trial on the issue. Not true. The appellate court has limited powers to review a case. For that reason, most trial court decisions are affirmed on appeal.

The bottom line: given the appellate court's limited basis of review, your chances of success are slim. But that's not to say it is impossible. And the chances of success increase depending on the issue being appealed. So check with an expert appellate lawyer next time you have been "wronged" by the trial court and see if you have any chance at beating the odds.

Standards for Appellate Review

The appellate court does not have the power to re-hear the case. Rather, the appellate court must adhere to one of three general standards when reviewing a case on appeal, and the two most commonly used standards are very difficult to meet for the appealing party. The three general appellate review standards are *de novo* review, substantial evidence, and abuse of discretion.

De novo review standard—de novo review is the best standard to use if you want to overturn a trial court decision, but it applies to very few appeals. *De novo* is Latin for "Do it over, Jack!" or rather, "Start from the beginning; anew." It applies to purely legal questions where the facts are undisputed by the parties. It allows the appellate court to consider the arguments anew, and they are not constrained by what the trial court found. For this reason, *de novo* review is the most favorable to the appealing party because they can argue the matter again as if a prior decision was not made.

Unfortunately, *de novo* review only applies to purely legal questions as opposed to rehashing the facts, documents, and testimony of your trial. For example, determining whether a California will requires one witness or two is a legal question based on California probate code. You do not need any case-specific facts to answer that question. Therefore, if the trial court said one witness is sufficient, when the statute requires two witnesses, then the appellate court can correct that decision on appeal using *de novo* review. When this occurs, the appellate court usually changes the trial court judgment that the trial court previously approved, and the case is over at that point.

Most trials involve many facts, documents, and witnesses, however, which generally must be accepted as true on appeal. In most cases, an appeal is going to argue about the evidence presented, not about a pure legal question. And for that reason, *de novo* review is rarely used.

Substantial evidence standard—this is not at all what you would think it is. Under this standard, the appellate court simply looks at the facts as decided by the trial court and determines if there is enough evidence to support those factual conclusions.

There are two steps to understanding the substantial evidence standard. First, the appellate court is required to assume that the factual decisions made by the judge or jury were accurate. The appellate court is NOT allowed to re-litigate or re-hear the case. In other words, if you think a witness lied on the stand, but the jury or judge took the witness' testimony as true, then the appellate court must also consider the witness' testimony is true when deciding whether to overturn the trial court ruling. The appellate court cannot re-try the case and decide for itself if the witness is truthful. The truthfulness of the witness has already been decided by the judge or jury, the appellate court's hands are tied. That means you are not going to win an appeal if your only gripe is that the witness lied on the witness stand. If the judge or jury believed the witness, then that's the truth for purposes of your case and for purposes of your appeal—you just have to live with it.

Second, given the "truth" as decided by the trial court, is there enough evidence to support the trial court's decision? If there is, then the trial court decision stands. If there is not, then the appellate court will either order a new trial at the trial court again, or the appellate court will issue a new judgment that replaces the prior judgment that was approved by the trial court.

In other words, this standard of review is not about whether the appellate court agrees with the trial court because that is irrelevant. Rather, it is just about whether the trial court had enough evidence on which to base its opinion. It does not have to be overwhelming evidence either, any old evidence will do. This is a very hard standard to meet on appeal, and for that reason most appellants will lose if they are stuck using this standard of review (and most appellants are stuck with this standard).

Most parties to a lawsuit, and many lawyers too, make the mistake of thinking the appellate court will right all wrongs of the trial court. That somehow the appellate court will see the lies and misinformation presented to the judge and jury and will strike down those lies to create a happy ending in the interests of truth and justice. Only in the movies does that occur. In real life, the appellate court must view the "truth" as it was decided by the judge and jury; it has no power to decide the truth for itself. The appellate court's only role under this standard of review is to ensure there is enough "truth" to support the judgment.

Abuse of discretion standard—this only applies in a matter where a trial court has the power to exercise discretion— meaning it can choose to do something or choose not do something—as opposed to a legally mandated decision. For example, in the case of awarding attorneys' fees where a trustee requests to be paid. Those types of fees are typically not set by statute. As such, the judge is given the power to decide what is reasonable under the circumstances of each case. If a judge awards a small amount of fees, and the trustee requested a large amount, then the trustee can appeal and claim that the trial court judge abused their discretion in reducing the fee request.

A trial court's decision will only be overturned on appeal if the trial court's action is a clear case of abuse of discretion and a miscarriage of justice. It is not enough that the trial court could have made a "better" decision. To be deemed "abuse," the trial court's action must exceed the bounds of reason when all circumstances are taken into account. It is not enough for the appellate court to have a different view of the matter. The appellate court may have given the trustee their entire fee request, but the appellate court is not allowed to consider that. The only question on appeal is "Did the trial court exceed all bounds of reason, or did it act arbitrarily and capricious?" If yes, then the appellate court can issue a different judgment or ask the trial court to reconsider the issues. If no, then the trial court decision stands. In other words, it is another tough standard to meet on appeal.

As you can see, appealing your trial court's decision is not so easy after all. But it helps to know what standard applies to you and then argue as best you can to meet that standard.

The end of your lawsuit is near. You have endured months, and probably years, of unexpected, chaotic legal wrangling, but you have survived, thanks to your flexibility, persistence, and resilience. There is just one last topic we should discuss if you have a trust or will lawsuit: no-contest clauses.

CHAPTER 17

The No-Contest Clause

This chapter only applies to a trust or will contest. If you have a civil case that does not involve a trust or will, then you can skip this chapter.

The no-contest clause can be a confusing area of trust law. Many lawyers do not fully understand the nuances of when no-contest clauses apply or how they should be used to defend a trust document. What's worse, many lawyers threaten to disinherit a beneficiary under a no-contest clause where the clause does not apply.

A no-contest clause is a trust provision that encourages beneficiaries NOT to file a trust or will contest lawsuit. The provision typically states that any beneficiary who challenges the validity of the trust or will in court shall be disinherited and receive no gift whatsoever under the trust or will. Historically, no-contest clauses were called *in terrorem* clauses— which is Latin for "to scare your socks off."

No-contest clauses have gone through many changes over the years under California law. The law has gradually limited the use of no-contest clauses and made their enforcement far more difficult than ever before.

The No-Contest Clause in California

In California, a no-contest clause in a trust or will is only enforced against three types of contests: (1) direct contests, (2) creditor's claims, and (3) contesting property ownership.

Direct Contests

A direct contest is defined as any pleading filed in court seeking to invalidate a trust or will document, or any of its terms, on the grounds of

- Forgery
- Lack of due execution
- Lack of capacity
- Undue influence
- Duress/menace
- Fraud

There are a few other grounds that would qualify as a direct contest, but they rarely occur and are not discussed here.

In most trust or will contest cases, a party is seeking to set aside a trust or will based on lack of capacity and/or undue influence. Those are two of the most used grounds for contesting a trust, trust amendment, will, or will codicil. As such, any document that contains a no-contest clause will likely be enforceable against a beneficiary who challenges the trust or will documents or any of its terms.

For example, assume that you are entitled to a specific gift of $250,000 under a trust, but under an earlier version of the trust you were named to receive half of the residue, which equals over $2 million. You believe the trust amendment that changed your gift from $2 million to $250,000 was signed by the settlor at a time when they lacked mental capacity, so you want to file a trust contest lawsuit to invalidate the last amendment to the trust (and, thereby, restore your gift of $2 million). If the trust contains a no-contest clause that pre-cludes direct contests, then your act of challenging the trust amendment in court will trigger the no-contest clause and likely cause you to lose your gift of $250,000 if you lose your trust contest lawsuit. If you win your lawsuit, then you would receive your original gift of $2 million. If you lose your lawsuit, then you receive nothing. You must decide, therefore, prior to filing suit whether you are willing to risk losing $250,000 to file your lawsuit.

The Probable Cause Exception

Luckily, there is an exception to enforcement of a no-contest clause against you where a direct contest is concerned. The exception applies where a beneficiary has probable cause to believe that the trust or will contest will be success-ful. In other words, if you have some facts that would lead a reasonable person to believe that the trust or will document, or some portion of it, is invalid, and you file your lawsuit on that basis, then you cannot be disinherited even if you lose the lawsuit.

Unfortunately, you do not know whether a court will agree that you had probable cause to file your lawsuit until AFTER you file your lawsuit. There is no longer a procedure to ob-tain the court's view on the matter prior to filing. But most courts, and most judges, would rather not disinherit a benefi-ciary. That means most courts will err on the side of caution and find that probable cause did exist at the time a trust or will contest was filed. This means that the likelihood of a beneficiary being disinherited after filing a direct contest of a trust or will is low. But you must treat this risk seriously all the same because you have no way of knowing how a court may rule in the future.

Typically, we advise all clients to assume that you will, in fact, be disinherited if you file your direct contest. As a result, you should make your decision on whether to proceed with a trust or will contest lawsuit with the risk of being disinherited in mind. Even with the risk of being disinherited, many clients still decide that the risk is worth taking and proceed with their trust or will contest lawsuit, but that is a personal decision that only you can make.

Creditor's Claims

No-contest clauses also apply to the filing of a creditor's claim or prosecution of an action based on it. This can be dangerous language because there are times when a beneficiary may cite a promise to be paid something from an estate as grounds for receiving a bigger share. Arguably, any pleading filed in court that asserts a legal claim to property based on a contract right could potentially trigger a trust or will no-contest clause.

The danger continues further because the filing of a creditor's claim, or the prosecution of an action based on it, is not protected by the probable cause exception discussed above. That means any time a contract right is asserted against a trust or will, it could potentially trigger the no-contest clause regardless of how much evidence the beneficiary had that the claim was valid.

In the case of a creditor's claim or the challenge of property ownership, a petition to enforce the no-contest clause can usually be brought much sooner. Both of these types of claims do not have the probable cause exception. And they both apply regardless of whether the underlying lawsuit is successful or not. They are elections, in other words, that allow the beneficiary to choose their own path. A beneficiary can choose to enforce a contract claim or to take under the terms of a trust or will, but the beneficiary cannot choose both. As such, the petition to enforce the no-contest clause can be filed immediately after the underlying lawsuit is filed.

Section 6 Brief

You need an experienced guide to help you wade through the no-contest clause thicket. At Albertson & Davidson, LLP, we have reviewed and analyzed thousands of no-contest clauses. While a no-contest clause may not stop you from suing, it must be considered and planned out if you hope to survive your lawsuit.

Let's consider what we have learned and how this knowledge will turn you into a flexible, persistent, and resilient litigation survivor.

CHAPTER 18

Your Guiding Light to Lawsuit Survival: Flexibility, Persistence, and Resilience

And there we have it, our tour of the American Litigation Process:

- The Pleading Phase
- The Discovery Phase: Written Discovery and Depositions
- The Mediation/Settlement Phase
- Other Pretrial Concerns: Terminating Motions and Expert Witnesses
- The Trial Phase
- For Trust or Will Contests: The No-Contest Clause

Many people find our court system frustrating and exhausting. That certainly can be true for many, but our judicial system is also marvelous. How so? It is one of the few systems in the world that offers a fair opportunity to resolve disputes among private citizens. Our court system is the great social equalizer. It is open to all, it allows an equal opportunity to be heard by all, and it provides an orderly method to resolve disputes.

Not only that, we have the jury system, which ensures your case will be decided by people in your community. This is a huge advantage to you because juries make different rulings from what judges would do. Not that judges are bad, it's just human nature. Juries are not professionals. They offer a fresh view of the process.

Every lawsuit has its ups and downs. One day good evidence will be discovered that makes the case better, and the next day bad evidence will come to light that makes the case look worse. The process can be an emotional roller coaster for everyone involved. The key is to persist. The good days are not as good as you think they are, and the bad days are not as bad as you think they are. At some point, a resolution will be reached. Often, the resolution comes in the form of a voluntary settlement. If not, then the resolution will come in the form of a decision made by a judge and/or jury. One way or another, your case will end.

In other words, there's light at the end of this tunnel. You may be happy with the resolution, or you may hate it, but life continues either way. And that's really the point: don't lose sight of how important your life is compared to your civil lawsuit. When the dust settles, and the lawsuit ends, your life continues. Lawsuits are not life and death, they just feel that way sometimes.

Hopefully, you now have some understanding of the process you are entering and what to expect from that process. It can be a long road, but you can successfully navigate it with some insight into how the process can work for you, insight that this book provides and that you will get with a little help from professionals like us at Albertson & Davidson, LLP: www.aldavlaw.com.

Glossary of Terms

Abuse of Discretion

An appellate standard that allows the appellate court to overturn a trial court decision if the trial court judge abused their discretion in reaching the decision.

Admit

A party's agreement with a particular fact.

Affirmative Defenses

Legal arguments made by the defendant (or responding party) that raise additional legal basis for why the defendant is not liable and should pay no damages in the lawsuit brought against the defendant.

Answer

When you pick up the telephone and say hello (you should already know this one). Also refers to the written document a defendant or respondent files with the court to respond to a civil complaint or petition.

Appeal

The process of asking the court of appeals (also referred to as the appellate court) to consider overturning a trial court's decision.

Arbitration

A process conducted outside of court to decide a lawsuit. Arbitration tends to be less formal than court. Arbitrations can be binding, meaning the decision is final and cannot be appealed (except in limited cases); or non-binding, meaning the parties can disregard the decision.

Authenticity

Refers to the genuineness of documents and other evidence to be used in court and/or during trial.

Authority, Legal

Legal authority means the statutory or case law that lawyers use to support the arguments they are making.

Bar

Establishment that serves alcohol to overworked lawyers. Also refers to the group of people who have been licensed to practice law.

Bench Trial	A trial that is heard and decided by a judge as opposed to a jury.
Beneficiary	The person or people who receive the assets of an estate.
Brief	A type of men's underwear. Also a written document that provides the law and facts necessary for the court to decide a given issue.
Business Records	A process of requesting and obtaining business documents from an **Subpoena** entity.
Business Records Subpoena	A process of requesting and obtaining business documents from an entity.
Capacity, Lack of	Most parents after a long day with the kids. Also the state of a person who is unable to make a decision or create a will because of a defect in their mental processing.

Case in Chief	A person's side of the lawsuit that is presented at trial. Each party has the opportunity to present their side of the lawsuit, which is then referred to as their case in chief.
Case Management Conference	A process where a civil court judge meets with the parties and/or their lawyers in court to determine the status of the case and whether a trial is ready to be set on the court's calendar.
Case Management Statement	A form document that is filled out and filed with the court prior to a case management conference to inform the judge of the status of the case.
Civil	Refers to being nice and polite to people. Also refers to any court case that does not involve criminal law.
Civil Case	Any court case that does not involve criminal law or criminal charges.

Civil Court	A department of the superior court that hears civil lawsuits, as opposed to criminal lawsuits. There is not a separate civil court; it actually is a department of the overall superior court system in California.
Civil Litigant	A person who is a party to a civil lawsuit. Litigant is just another term for a party to a lawsuit.
Closing Argument	The statement made to the jury at the end of trial that explains your side of the case and attempts to persuade the jury to rule in your favor.
Code of Civil Procedure	A set of California laws that pertains to civil lawsuits. The California Code of Civil Procedure includes the Discovery Act too, which governs the use of civil discovery in lawsuits.

Complaint	The initial written document that starts a civil lawsuit. The complaint is supposed to state the basic factual allegations and the legal basis on which the lawsuit is based.
Consumer's Notice	A process of notifying consumers whenever a party attempts to obtain personal and private records, such as bank statements, medical records, and similar information. A consumer's notice must be issued on every individual whose personal information is seeking to be obtained by a party to a lawsuit.
Continuance	Refers to rescheduling anything in your lawsuit to a later date. For example, a hearing continuance means the hearing will take place on a future date.
Court Reporter	The stenographer who sits in on every deposition and takes shorthand notes of everything anyone says during the deposition. Court reporters are also used in

most courtrooms during hearings and trial.

Creditor's Claim

A document filed in a probate estate that notifies the court and all people interested in that estate that they have a claim that needs to be paid.

Cross-Examination

Usually the second person to ask questions of a witness is engaging in a cross examination.

Custodian of Records

The person who is in charge of maintaining the business records for any entity.

Default

Refers to when you can't find the one you love, so you love the one you're with. Also refers to the court clerk entering a notation on your court case indicating no answer has been filed by the defendant, thereby, allowing the plaintiff to ask for a default judgment.

Default Judgment

A judgment entered by the court after a party fails to answer, so a default is entered.

Defendant

The party who must respond to a lawsuit. The person being sued.

Demurrer

A written document where a party asks the court to dismiss the lawsuit based solely on what is stated in the complaint or petition.

Denial

Not just a river in Egypt. Also refers to the process in discovery where the request to admit a fact is denied.

De Novo

Refers to an appellate court's power to review and decide a legal issue on its own without having to defer to the prior decision of the trial court. De novo means the appellate court can hear the issue anew.

Deposition

A process where a witness is asked questions by a lawyer while under oath and with a court reporter present to record everything that is said.

Direct Contest

Refers to a lawsuit that seeks to overturn a trust or will based on limited legal theories, such as undue influence, lack of capacity, and fraud.

Direct Examination

Usually the first person to ask questions of a witness is engaging in direct examination.

Discovery

The process of obtaining information and evidence after your lawsuit is filed, but before trial.

Discovery Act

The set of laws contained within the California Code of Civil Procedures that governs the process of obtaining information and evidence after your lawsuit has been filed, but before trial.

Discovery Motion

A written document filed with the court asking that the court issue an order to enforce the rules under the Discovery Act. Discovery motions are often brought when a party refuses or fails to comply with their obligations in responding to discovery.

Disinherited

A person who was once potentially entitled to receive assets from an estate, but has since been excluded from receiving anything.

Document Demand

The process under the Discovery Act that allows a party to a lawsuit to obtain documents and other information from another party to the same lawsuit.

Document Production

The process of providing documents or other information to another party in a lawsuit when compelled to do so under a document demand.

Due Process of Law

The legal process that forms the cornerstone of common law judicial systems whereby each party to a lawsuit is given an equal chance to be heard.

Duress

Forcing a person to take an action, or not take an action, by using forceful means.

Evidence	Testimony, documents, and other information that are used at trial (and during other parts of a lawsuit) to support a desired result.
Evidence Code	The set of rules in California that governs the use of information during trial.
Evidence, Rules of	The rules set forth under the Evidence Code. See Evidence Code.
Examination	Asking questions of a witness. See Cross-Examination and Direct Examination.
Examination, Cross	See Cross-Examination.
Examination, Direct	See Direct Examination.
Ex Parte	A single party to a lawsuit. Also refers to a hearing that is brought on an emergency basis with short notice or no notice to the other parties to the lawsuit.
Ex Parte Communications	When a single party to a lawsuit attempts to communicate with the court or judge without the other party present. Ex parte

	communications are generally prohibited.
Expert Witness	A person, usually paid by a party, who provides testimony about a complex issue involved in the lawsuit.
Forgery	A faked signature.
Form Interrogatory	A set of questions provided on a pre-printed form by the California Judicial Council. A party need only check the appropriate boxes to complete a set of form interrogatories.
Foundation	The process of authenticating evidence or providing some basis for which questions will later be asked.
Fraud	The act of knowingly taking advantage of a person for personal gain by either lying about a pertinent fact or intentionally omitting a pertinent fact.
General Denial	Your children's answer to every question about who broke something. Also refers to the form document that allows a defendant to

simply deny all allegations in a complaint as the initial response to a lawsuit.

Hearing

When the parties and their lawyers appear in court to discuss some aspect of the case with the judge.

Hearsay

An evidentiary rule that is meant to prevent gossip from entering the trial system. Legally speaking, hearsay is any out-of-court statement that is used during trial to prove a fact.

Information and Belief

An allegation in a complaint or petition that is not known with certainty by the party making the allegation, but they think it might be correct.

In Personam

Refers to a type of legal jurisdiction that requires the presence of a specific person or entity in court in order to properly resolve a lawsuit. Most civil lawsuits require in personam jurisdiction.

In Rem

Refers to a type of legal jurisdiction that focuses on a specific piece of property, or group of assets, which does not require the presence of a specific person or entity in court in order to properly resolve a lawsuit. When the court handles a probate, that is a classic example of in rem jurisdiction.

Inspection Demand

See Document Demand.

Interrogatory

A set of written questions presented to a party to a lawsuit. The party receiving a set of interrogatories is expected to respond to them in writing.

In Terrorem Clause

To scare the pants off your bratty kids. Also the Latin term that refers to a no-contest clause, meaning if a beneficiary to a trust or will attempts to invalidate the document, they will be disinherited and receive nothing.

Intestate

A person who dies without a will. Also refers to the set of laws contained in the California Probate Code that governs the administration of estates for people who die without a will.

Judge

The person who is in charge of the courtroom to which your lawsuit is assigned.

Judgment

When people tell you your shoes don't match your out-fit. Also refers to the final determination of your law-suit. A judgment is the legal paper that gives the win-ning party the right either to collect what they are owed or to have a final de-termination that nothing is owed, depending on the outcome of the lawsuit.

Jurisdiction

The legal right a particular court has to resolve a given lawsuit. Jurisdiction can re-fer to both the parties to the lawsuit (the court must have the ability to force each of the parties to par-ticipate in the lawsuit) and the subject matter of the lawsuit (the court must have the power to decide the issues raised by the law-suit).

Jury	A group of citizens who are empaneled with the authority to decide the facts of your lawsuit. Juries are often referred to as the trier of facts because they decide which facts will be believed and used for resolving your lawsuit.
Lack of Capacity	See Capacity, Lack of.
Lack of Due Execution	Execution, or executed, is how lawyers refer to signatures. Lack of due execution refers to a document that either was not signed or was not signed properly as required under California law. For example, a California will must be signed by the will creator and two witnesses. If the will was signed by the creator but no witnesses, then the will would be invalid because it lacks due execution.
Leave to Amend	A court's grant of permission to allow a party to a lawsuit to amend their complaint or petition.
Legal Authority	The set of laws and prior court cases that lawyers use

to support the rulings they are asking the court to make.

Litigation

The process of conducting a lawsuit.

Mail Service

The process of notifying parties to a lawsuit by mailing them documents.

Mandatory Settlement

A court process where all parties are required to appear in person and conference to try to voluntarily settle the lawsuit.

Mediation

A private process that takes place outside of court where the parties personally appear and attempt to voluntarily settle the lawsuit.

Mediator

Jan Brady, or any middle child in a family of three or more children. Also refers to the neutral professional who is paid to work with the parties at mediation to try to reach a voluntary settlement of the lawsuit.

Menace	Dennis, the. Also refers to forcing a person to take an action, or not take an action, by using threat or forceful means.
Motion for Judgment on the Pleadings	A written document filed with the court asking the court to dismiss on the Pleadings the lawsuit based solely on what is stated in the documents filed by the plaintiff or petitioner in their complaint/petition.
Motion for Summary Adjudication	A written document filed with the court asking the court to rule against on certain evidence, or lack of evidence, obtained by the parties, along with what is stated in the complaint or petition. Summary adjudication refers to the court deciding a single issue in a lawsuit, as opposed to ruling on the entire lawsuit.
Motion for Summary Adjudication	A written document filed with the court asking the court to rule against on certain evidence, or lack of evidence, obtained by the parties, along with what is stated in the complaint or

petition. Summary judgment refers to the court deciding the entire lawsuit as opposed to just a single issue in the lawsuit.

Motion in Limine	Refers to a written document filed with the court before trial starts asking the court to prohibit certain actions.
Motion to Compel	See Discovery Motion.
Motion to Strike	A written document filed with the court asking the court to delete a small portion of the text of a complaint or petition.
No-Contest Clause	See In Terrorem Clause.
Notice	The process of notifying parties to a lawsuit about filings and future hearings pertaining to the lawsuit.
Notice of Hearing	The process of notifying parties to a lawsuit about future hearings scheduled in the lawsuit.
Notice of Motion	The process of notifying parties to a lawsuit about future dates when the court will decide a motion.

Objection

When a party, or their attorney, voices a problem with a given question that is being asked. Objections can also be used in written form in response to discovery requests.

Opening Statement

The process of talking to the judge or jury at the outset of a trial to inform them of what evidence will be brought in the upcoming trial.

Order

Your spouse's final decision on an issue. Also a written document issued by the court that obligates a party to a lawsuit to take a certain action or refrain from taking a certain action.

Overrule

When a judge disagrees with an objection and allows a question to be answered.

Party

What you do after you win your lawsuit. Also refers to a person or entity that has either been named in a lawsuit or has voluntarily joined a lawsuit.

Party to a Lawsuit

Refers to a person or entity that has either been named in a lawsuit or has voluntarily joined a lawsuit.

Penalty of Perjury

Refers to the legal consequences that can arise for a party who lies while under oath.

Personal Service

The process of notifying someone by personally handing them documents as opposed to mailing documents to them.

Petition

A written document filed with the court that seeks a court order on an issue. Most probate court filings are done in the form of a petition.

Petitioner

The person who files a petition in court.

Plaintiff

The person who files a complaint in civil court to begin the lawsuit.

Pleadings

The written documents filed by all parties through the life of the lawsuit are referred to collectively as the "pleadings" or "written pleadings."

Post-Trial Motions

Any written document filed after a trial is concluded seeking an order from the court. Usually refers to a motion that seeks to change the decision made by the judge or jury.

Probable Cause

The legal basis by which a court can choose to excuse an action that would otherwise lead to disinheritance under a no-contest clause.

Probate

The court process used to oversee the orderly transfer of assets from a deceased person to their rightful heirs or beneficiaries.

Probate Court

A department of the Superior Court that hears matters brought under the California Probate Code, as opposed to criminal lawsuits. There is not a separate probate court; it actually is a department of

the overall superior court
system in California.

Probate Petition

The initial written document filed by a party seeking to start the process of probate.

Property Rights

Refers to a person's legal rights to either receive or retain assets.

Reply

A written document where a party provides their rebuttal argument to a response. Typically, a reply is used to support a motion.

Request for Admission

A discovery document that allows one party to a lawsuit to ask another party to admit certain facts are true.

Request for Production

See Document Demand.

Respondent

The person who responds to a petition.

Response

A written document where a party provides their rebuttal argument to a motion filed by another party.

Service, Mail	See Mail Service.
Service of Process	The method a person uses to provide documents and information to a party to the lawsuit.
Service, Personal	See Personal Service.
Settlement	A voluntary resolution to end a lawsuit.
Settlement Agreement	A written document that sets forth the terms of which the parties have voluntarily agreed to resolve the lawsuit.
Special Interrogatory	A set of written questions that are drafted by a party or their attorney.
Statute of Limitations	The rules that govern the deadlines by which a lawsuit must be filed.
Subpoena	The legal mechanism parties and their lawyers used to obtain testimony and written documents from people and entities who are not parties to the lawsuit.

Substantial Evidence   An appellate standard that requires the appellate court to confirm a trial court ruling unless the trial court's ruling did not have enough evidentiary support.

Summary Adjudication   See Motion for Summary Adjudication.

Summary Judgment   See Motion for Summary Judgment.

Summons   A written document issued by the clerk of the court that obligates a party to a lawsuit to appear and respond to the lawsuit.

Supplemental Response   A further written response to discovery that either provides more information or removes unwarranted objections.

Sustain   A judge's decision to agree with a given objection and prevent a question from being answered.

Testate   A person who dies having created a will before death is said to have died testate.

Testator	A person who creates a will.
Testimony	A statement given by a witness either during deposition or at trial.
Testimony, Live	See Testimony. Live testimony refers to someone speaking as opposed to a written statement.
Transcript	The process whereby the parties are allowed to present evidence, argue their case, and obtain a final decision.
Trust	An estate planning document whereby a person's assets are transferred to another (the trustee) to hold, manage, and safeguard until such time that the assets transfer to the beneficiaries.
Trust Contest	A legal process where a person attempts to invalidate a trust or a trust amendment.
Trustee	A person who manages a trust. The trustee is the legal owner of the property, which gives the trustee the

power and authority to control the trust assets.

Under Oath   The legal recitation that in-
dicates that any statement
made in person, or in writing, must be truthful otherwise the speaker could face
criminal charges.

Undue Influence   Coercive behavior that
causes the replacement of a
person's own intent with
the intent of another.

Verification   A written document that a
party signs confirming that
any facts stated in the document are true. Verification
must be signed under pen-
alty of perjury, meaning any
intentionally false statements in the document
could subject the signer to
criminal penalties.

Verified Complaint A complaint that is filed
with a verification attached
to it. See Complaint and
Verification.

Verified Petition   A petition that is filed with a
verification attached to it.
See Petition and Verification.

Will	A written document that sets forth a person's intention for the final distribution of their assets after death.
Will Contest	A legal process where a person attempts to invalidate a will or a will amendment (referred to as a will codicil).
Witness	A person who will give information under oath. Also refers to someone who is present when a will is signed by the testator (will creator) and then signs the will to evidence they were present and watched the will being signed.
Witness, Fact	A person who has personal knowledge of the facts or circumstances of a lawsuit.
Witness, Percipient	Same as Fact Witness.
Written Discovery	Each of the techniques allowed under the Discovery Act where a party can obtain a written response from another party to the same lawsuit.

About the Firm

Founded in 2008, Albertson & Davidson, LLP, serves abused beneficiaries who are facing financial battles over trusts, wills, and probate matters. Our team of seven estate attorneys has extensive courtroom experience successfully litigating complex and often emotionally charged legal issues.

At Albertson & Davidson, LLP, we are driven by compassion for our clients. We understand the frustration and panic that sets in when you realize someone has been stealing from your heritage or manipulating a situation for their own financial gain. We know how hot emotions can run and how families can be forever divided in long-running arguments over wills, trusts, and financial elder abuse proceedings.

Our aggressive trust and will trial lawyers have extensive experience navigating sensitive situations and successfully securing the satisfactory outcomes our clients deserve. Our firm is strictly focused on this complex area of law, and our trial attorneys have honed their skills in courtrooms all across California. We stand, we fight, and we win.

With offices in Los Angeles, San Francisco, San Diego County, Orange County, and Silicon Valley, our firm is available to assist clients throughout California. We offer free consultations, and if we can't take your case, we will refer you to someone who can.

If you or a loved one's financial future is on the line, you need to take action now to protect your legal rights. Contact us now to discuss your case and set up a complimentary case evaluation with our team.

Website: https://www.aldavlaw.com/

Email: keith@aldavlaw.com and stewart@aldavlaw.com

Phone: 1–877–632–1738

About the Authors

Keith A. Davidson is managing partner of Albertson & Davidson, LLP. Originally from Denver, Colorado, Keith attended Loyola Law School in Los Angeles, where he served as the Note and Comment Editor for the *Loyola International and Comparative Law Review* before graduating in the top ten percent of his class.

Keith A. Davidson

With nearly two decades of experience in California trust, will, estate, and probate litigation, Keith has passionately sought to help clients throughout California resolve their legal problems and enjoys thinking creatively to position cases for success at trial. He also enjoys exploring legal topics through his monthly articles in the firm's trust, estate, and probate litigation blog.

Stewart R. Albertson received his law degree from Loyola University New Orleans School of Law before obtaining an LLM degree in taxation from Georgetown University Law Center in Washington, DC. Prior to attending law school, Stewart served as a paratrooper in the 82nd Airborne Division of the United States Army for two years, and before that was stationed along the DMZ border of North Korea and South Korea for a one-year tour with the Second Infantry Division.

Stewart R. Albertson

With a focus on energetic and dynamic representation committed to achieving just and fair results for his clients, Stewart has helped the firm's clients obtain over $100 million in verdicts and settlements, including a jury verdict in one San Bernardino wrongful death case for $5.7 million (Sloan v. Redmond).

Index

Made in the USA
Thornton, CO
10/04/24 02:12:15

624f9aef-0a5c-4244-ac56-ebf324c0f7fdR01